Intimate Moments

❤

DAILY DEVOTIONS
FOR COUPLES

INTIMATE MOMENTS

♥

DAILY DEVOTIONS
FOR COUPLES

David and Teresa Ferguson
Chris and Holly Thurman

A JANET THOMA BOOK

THOMAS NELSON PUBLISHERS
Nashville

Published in Nashville, Tennessee, by Thomas Nelson, Inc.,
and distributed in Canada by Lawson Falle, Ltd., Cambridge,
Ontario.

Scripture quotations are from the NEW KING JAMES
VERSION of the Bible. Copyright © 1979, 1980, 1982,
Thomas Nelson, Inc., Publishers. Scripture quotations noted
NASB are taken from THE NEW AMERICAN STANDARD
BIBLE, Copyright © 1960, 1962, 1963, 1968, 1971, 1972,
1973, 1975, 1977 by The Lockman Foundation and are used
by permission.

Library of Congress Cataloging-in-Publication Data

Intimate moments : daily devotions for couples / by David and
   Teresa Ferguson, Chris and Holly Thurman.
     p.   cm.
  ISBN 0-8407-4568-0
    1. Married people—Prayer-books and devotions—English.
2. Devotional calendars.   3. Intimacy (Psychology)—
Religious aspects—Christianity—Meditations. I. Ferguson,
David, 1947–   .
BV4596.M3I58   1993
242′.644—dc20   92-25524
                                      CIP

Printed in the United States of America
1 2 3 4 5 6 — 98 97 96 95 94 93

Introduction

Intimacy doesn't just happen without effort, neither can it be programmed to happen. Couples grow in closeness as they encounter each other spiritually, emotionally, and physically. An ecstatic moment of common joy, a tearful sharing of genuine apology, an affectionate embrace—through intimate moments such as these, couples deepen their marital intimacy.

Intimacy can't be scientifically measured, as our temperature can. Rather we feel it; it's a subjective experience. Because each of us feels differently, we experience intimacy in different ways. One person might feel close while enjoying a quiet walk, holding hands with his spouse, while another might feel intimate working with her mate on a household project.

Each of us has unique relational or "intimacy" needs that, when met, produce closeness and feelings of being loved. For example, the emotional feelings of love are often related to our needs for attention, affection, and appreciation being met. As we come to better understand our spouses' significant relational needs, we will be better equipped to love them. As we are reminded of God's abundant giving to us, we are prompted from within to give to others.

Beginning with our need for acceptance, we've identified 52 areas of need in these devotionals—one for each week—that, when met, deepen intimacy and heighten felt love in the marriage relationship. We talk about the ways God has met our needs, as well as the ways we can give to each other. We've included personal reflections and stories from our counseling. And at the close of each week, we have a devotional of practical application.

May God richly bless your exploration of deepened intimacy with Him and your marriage partner.

ACCEPTANCE—DELIBERATE, UNCONDITIONAL, AND POSITIVE

*Therefore receive one another, just as Christ
also received us.*
　　　　　　　　　　　—ROM. 15:7

*A*cceptance is the basis of my knowledge of Christ.
When God allowed Christ to die in my behalf, He made
a *deliberate* choice. In coming to "seek and save the
lost," Christ took the initiative. He looks beyond my
actions and sins to accept me as I am; this *unconditional* acceptance is *permanent*—there's nothing I can
do to merit it or to lose it!

　　God accepted me when He looked beyond my faults
to see my need. This "looking beyond" makes marriage work, too—looking beyond differences, disagree-
ments, and disputes; looking beyond irritations,
personalities, and idiosyncrasies; looking beyond
wrongs, faults, and sin . . . not to excuse them, but to
see worth in my spouse in spite of them.

▼　　*Please grant me the divine gift of "looking beyond"
in order to see my spouse's best qualities.*

ACCEPTANCE BEGINS WITH GOD

*"Shall we indeed accept good from God, and
shall we not accept adversity?"*
—JOB 2:10

*M*y wife is so different from me: always on time, a perfectionist, outgoing. When things go wrong, those differences make her seem impatient, critical, and loud—qualities that are difficult for me to accept.

But acceptance doesn't mean condoning behavior; it means looking deeper, just as God sees my sin and looks deeper. His divine love is able to separate my worth from my behavior. God may declare my sin, but He also declares that I am more than my sin. Because Christ died in my place, my worth is infinite. His acceptance of me is permanent. I haven't done anything to gain it, so I can't do anything to lose it!

Gradually, I have come to look beyond Teresa's manner, and my gratitude for her as a special and loving helpmate continues to grow. Truly, "he who finds a wife finds a good thing, and obtains favor with the Lord" (Prov. 18:22).

▼ *Lord, may my gratitude for Your acceptance of me prompt within me today a joyful acceptance of my spouse.*

I'M A 10

For by one offering He has perfected forever those who are being sanctified.
—HEB. 10:14

I had always been critical of myself and others rather than accepting, as Christ is. I thought that by conforming to the world's standards of what is acceptable—right clothes, right weight, right job, etc.—I would be loved and accepted by God as well as others.

Then God showed me how wrong my thinking was. I'd said some really hurtful things to David, and I knew I needed to confess to God and ask for forgiveness. As I was telling God how bad I'd been, He very gently said, "I know. You're forgiven." "Wait! That was too easy, God. Let me tell You again." But again He said, "You're forgiven, Teresa. I knew what you would do and not do from the beginning of time, and I still want you and accept you." When I heard God's truth—that He already knows my sins and accepts me anyway—a burden lifted. I don't have to do anything to be worthy. God sees me as worthy because of Christ's death.

▼ *The world says if you perform perfectly, you're a 10. My formula is this:*
Christ = 1; my performance = 0; 1 + 0 = 10.
I am a 10 with Christ.

ACCEPTANCE IN A SYCAMORE TREE

"Zacchaeus, make haste and come down, for today I must stay at your house."
—LUKE 19:5

Zacchaeus, a hated tax-collector, a traitor to his own people, and a thief, was no doubt often ridiculed and attacked for his sins. Lonely and curious, he climbed a tree to get a good look at this "Messiah." Would Jesus notice him? And if He did, would He, too, reject him? What a miracle Christ's call must have been! Attacking another's behavior is a common "fleshly" response. To *accept*, as Christ did with Zacchaeus, is the exception rather than the rule.

When we ask couples to keep a diary of their complaints about each other, they are often shocked by its size. Then it is easy to see that sharing needs and meeting them is more constructive than complaining. What a difference between (1) "You've worked every night this week and I'm tired of it!" which attacks, and (2) "I really sense how hard you've been working, and at the same time I find myself missing you. Could we plan some special time for just us?" which expresses need.

▼ *Please help me shift my focus from reacting to others' behavior to sharing my needs and giving to the needs of others.*

JUST AS I AM

"He who receives you receives Me, and he who receives Me receives Him who sent Me."
—MATT. 10:40

I grew up in a military family that valued discipline and order. In our house, there was a place for everything and everything was in its place. My wife's family was much more laid-back—they left things all over their house, rarely noticing. When we married, our two styles clashed like brown shoes with a tuxedo.

I'd come home from work and find Holly's coat on the chair, her car keys on top of the washer, her purse on the bed, and her shoes in the middle of the living room floor. I didn't respond well to her "mess." In fact, I was pretty obnoxious about it.

God, as He often does, showed me that, though I thought Holly had the problem, I had the bigger one. My intolerance was a "plank in my eye," whereas her behavior was a speck in her's.

I still trip over shoes left in the middle of the living room floor, but now they remind me to accept Holly as she is rather than to try to make her like me. Funny thing—the more I've accepted Holly, the more she has changed.

 God, help me accept my spouse as he or she is and focus on my own problems.

CONDITIONAL OR UNCONDITIONAL? THAT IS THE QUESTION!

Therefore receive one another, just as Christ also received us. —ROM. 15:7

The muscles in the back of my neck tightened with each complaint. "But he won't lead! He's not spiritual enough! He's made a mess out of our finances!" The list was endless. It seemed to always end this way with visits to my friend Laura: She would dump all her marital woes on me, and I would leave with a headache. But why? Maybe there was some painful parallel between us that I didn't want to see.

There was. God helped me to see that both Laura and I were accepting our husbands conditionally. When she criticized her husband and used his shortcomings as an excuse to not love him, it was a painful look in the mirror at my critical behavior with my husband, Chris.

God loves us as we are because we are His creation. In Christ, He accepts us unconditionally. Trying to accept our spouses as God accepts us is difficult—sometimes like trying to climb Mount Everest. But as impossible as it may seem, with God's help, and only with God's help, it is possible to accept our spouses, warts and all. Without God's help, it will only remain a dream.

▼ *Thank You, God, for Your unconditional and permanent acceptance. Help me to accept my spouse as Christ accepted me.*

ACCEPTING AN IMPERFECT PERSON

God demonstrates His own love toward us, in that while we were still sinners, Christ died for us.
                                        —ROM. 5:8

$\mathcal{M}$ost couples go through stages in their marriage before they reach Romantic Realism—the stage where you're loving a real person, an admittedly imperfect person. Where do you see yourself?

Romantic Stage—*You're perfect, ideal, and everything I need!*

Bargaining Stage—You're sure *not* perfect, and I'll change if you will.

Coercive Stage—Like it or not, I'm going to change you! And if I need help, I'll sic God on you.

Desperation Stage—You'll never change—I give up—I quit (either physically or emotionally).

Acceptance Stage—Frankly both of us are kind of strange; neither of us is perfect—but I'm sure committed to you.

Every time we repeat the following vow to each other, we move closer to Romantic Realism:

I take you to be my spouse with full knowledge that you will disappoint me gravely—that you will hurt me deeply. In spite of all this, I commit myself to love you knowing your weakness and the certainty of your failure!

▼ *Heavenly Father, keep me reminded of what love really is: Love—An unconditional commitment to an imperfect person.*

ADMONITION—CONSTRUCTIVE GUIDANCE

You also are full of goodness, . . . knowledge,
able also to admonish one another.
                                    —ROM. 15:14

*L*ike the proverbial sheep, I tend to wander amidst the conflicting pulls on my life, and I often rejoice that I've not been left without God's admonitions! The Great Shepherd has promised that His Spirit will guide and His Word will direct. Because of His love for me, He warns me—in His word and through the grieving within me of His Spirit. I'm sure He knows and loves me.

I gain a great sense of security through the knowledge of God's admonition: His Word and Spirit serve as guardrails for life's journey.

▼ *Father, make my heart sensitive to Your admonishing voice.*

ADMONITION IN THE GARDEN

> *The day you eat of [this tree], you shall surely die.*
> —GEN. 2:17

$\mathcal{R}$emember God's admonition to Adam? How loving it was for God to warn him! Imagine another scene: Adam is in the Garden surrounded by the fullness of God's creation. He wants to eat, but God says: "There's one tree out there with poison fruit, but I won't tell you which one!" Would you serve that kind of God? As we travel the narrow path that leads to life, God's admonition is always clear and for our best interest.

Admonition never accuses or shames. Instead, it should communicate love and concern. The bedrock of a successful marriage is the trust that one's spouse shows concern, or warns out of love. In this way, we keep relationships "approachable," open, and secure.

▼ *Father, help us to share our concerns lovingly and openly.*

PICKY, PICKY, PICKY

"And why do you look at the speck in your brother's eye, but do not consider the plank in your own eye?"
—MATT. 7:3

To give constructive guidance in what to avoid; to warn." That definition of *admonition* has a *positive* feel to it. I certainly had the best intentions when I warned David about the speed traps lurking around the next turn in the road. Unfortunately, David didn't receive my admonitions as positive or constructive guidance! But when I finally decided that God could do the admonishing, I stopped trying to control David's driving. I discovered that not only was he more responsive to my warnings, I was freer to focus on all the things he does right.

▼ *God, thank You for reminding me that I am responsible only for my own actions.*

ADMONITION—I DON'T NEED IT!

I do not write these things to shame you, but as my beloved children I warn you.
—1 COR. 4:14

"Sweetheart, do you really want to go down the Interstate?" It was an innocent enough question. Teresa was just trying to be helpful so that we could be on time for our social engagement. So why did I react with such quick anger? "I'll get us there," was my sharp, sarcastic response.

Admonition is one of those needs that I resist needing! To me, constructive guidance implies that I don't know everything, that my way is not perfect, and this truth is hard to swallow. My fleshly nature fights admonition no matter how lovingly it's conveyed. What if my wife's admonition had been even more personal? "Honey, I'm really concerned about our lack of unity in disciplining the kids. Could we plan a time to discuss it?" Could I receive such a concern gracefully? Or would I attack, blaming and defensive? I saw that I needed to ask God to make me more like Christ in spirit.

▼ *Father, as You see things about my life that contradict Christ's message, use someone, including my spouse, to lovingly point them out to me.*

WARNING—TROUBLE AHEAD!

The humble He guides in justice, and the
humble He teaches His way.   —PS. 25:9

*H*ave you ever noticed how many warning signs there are in life? DO NOT ENTER; DON'T WALK; CAUTION—DANGER AHEAD. All are designed to help us avoid things that would hurt us. We have a difficult time heeding warnings, though.

We see CAUTION—ICE ON BRIDGE, and speed on, only to slide out of control.

Often husbands and wives ignore early warning signs in marriage, allowing small, easy-to-handle problems to become huge, overwhelming problems.

One spouse may pick up on a problem and sound the alarm. But the other often doesn't see the problem or resists the warnings.

We need to guide each other constructively through marriage. We need to listen when being warned rather than get defensive and shutting down. At Pearl Harbor, radar indicated that planes were on the way but was ignored. Don't allow a "Pearl Harbor" in your marriage. Read the warning signs, tell each other, and respond quickly.

▼ *God, help us to notice the early warning signs in our marriage, and to lovingly alert each other so we can take constructive action.*

WHERE DO YOUR LOYALTIES LIE?

*A wise man will hear and increase learning,
and a man of understanding will attain wise
counsel.*
                                    —PROV. 1:5

*M*y family had just left after a four-day visit. I'd had
a great time seeing everybody! But Chris looked unhappy, as he often had during their visit.

"Sweetheart," I asked, "what's bothering you?"
Chris answered that whenever my family was around he
felt demoted to last place on my totem pole. He felt I
acted more like a daughter and a sister to my family
than like his wife. When I sat and talked with my family,
I acted as if he wasn't there, so he felt left out.

My immediate response was defensive. He was being
too sensitive, I told myself. After all, I didn't get to see
my family much, and I saw him all the time. But I could
see that all my excuses wouldn't make the hurt in his
eyes go away.

Right then I determined to be more caring toward
Chris during family visits. I made sure he was included
in everything, especially conversations. And I made a
point of sitting by him every chance I could.

God faithfully showed me that Chris is my husband
and my family now, and needs to be my top priority.
Chris's constructive feedback, though painful, helped
correct some insensitivity in me that needed to be corrected.

▼ *God, help me accept my spouse's guidance and direction to stay on track!*

ADMONITION—MARRIAGE GOALS

*Can two walk together, unless they are
agreed?*
—AMOS 3:3

*A*greeing on where you're going is essential to oneness in relationships. It can start with the simple rule
that neither spouse makes a commitment involving the
other without discussing it first. Other goals might include a weekly family night, remodeling plans, or vacation ideas, each of which encourages "walking
together" as a couple or family.

Remember the satisfaction you feel when you've
checked each item off your "things-to-do" list? Your life
is not out of control; instead, you've taken charge of
your destiny. Setting goals for marriage and family can
have the same effect, multiplied many times over. And
accomplishing those goals can bring a deep sense of
togetherness to each family member.

Spend time together reflecting on: *What do we hope
to accomplish in our marriage and family during the
next year?*

▼ *Give us a clear vision, heavenly Father, of how we
might walk together in Your light.*

AFFECTION—COMMUNICATING CLOSENESS THROUGH TOUCH

Greet one another with a holy kiss.
—ROM. 16:16

*O*f the five senses, touch is one we need most. Lack of caring touch actually hinders development in newborns. Caring touch not only nurtures security in a child, it communicates worth and value to everyone. Caring touch diminishes the fear of intimacy and deepens trust.

The sixty seconds it takes to greet one another after a long day are probably the most important you'll spend. As a general rule, a warm and tender embrace will help set the atmosphere for the evening hours.

▼ *Lord, help me to remember the importance of a warm and tender greeting.*

AFFECTION DURING THE PASSOVER MEAL

> ... *leaning back on Jesus' breast.*
> —JOHN 13:25

$\mathcal{A}$s the time of His departure nears, Jesus reveals the troubling news about His betrayal, about His death. John may not know exactly how to help, but the beloved disciple draws closer to his Master. How can I support a loved one in pain, particularly when there seems to be no way I can fix it? It may seem inadequate at first, but touch can say *"I care"* and *"I'm here."* During trouble and pain, there's no greater message than that.

Many a marriage could benefit from more caring touch, especially "friendship" touching: holding hands on a walk, an arm around the shoulder during church, or a gentle pat at the dinner table.

▼ *Father, sensitize my heart to my partner's need for caring, and to the power of gentle touch.*

FEARING AFFECTION

Perfect love casts out fear.
—1 JOHN 4:18

I really feared affection, for two reasons. The first source was my family, a large one of six kids. Though I know Mom and Dad loved us—Mom cooked our favorite food and Dad went to work—they didn't tell us so or hug us. The second source was unhealed hurts that occurred when David and I were first married.

My fears eventually became a problem in our marriage. David was raised in a small (two kids), affectionate family. When he'd come home wanting a hug, I'd want to make him a roast or a pie. Because of all our unhealed hurts, I also had difficulty giving sexually. When God started healing the hurts from our childhood and we started healing our hurts with each other, my fears slowly melted away.

Affection seemed unnatural to me at first, but now I need it. God has changed me in ways that have deepened our relationship and actually freed me to enjoy affection!

▼ *God, thank You for Your perfect love, which casts out my fears.*

AFFECTION—WHY WASTE IT!

*Then the LORD said to me, "Go again, love a
woman who is loved by her husband."*
—HOS. 3:1

*C*laim me when we're out in public!" was a common
complaint early in our marriage. In a new social setting,
I would often leave Teresa to fend for herself. I might
withdraw to a quiet corner with a colleague, or escape
into a work-related conversation with a few friends;
Teresa felt rejected and ignored. I felt it was *her* problem. For a time, it was a painful issue for both of us.

Affection was the answer. Teresa needs to know that I
enjoy being with her, and that I am proud she is my
wife. Giving her my arm or holding her hand as we walk
reminds her of my love. At first I felt awkward "wast-
ing" physical affection, since it wasn't leading anywhere. But I tried it—and it worked. Teresa feels more
secure and I feel less selfish, more giving.

 *Today, help me think more about others and less
about myself.*

CAN A ZEBRA CHANGE ITS STRIPES?

Greet one another with a holy kiss.
—1 COR. 16:20

I am not naturally affectionate. My wife, Holly, is. She likes to hold hands and whisper sweet nothings. I like to keep my feelings inside and be "The Lone Ranger."

What a bad match, you may say. What a *great* match, I say. God hooked me up with a very affectionate person to change me. He has used Holly to help me grow comfortable with my feelings and expressing them toward others.

Am I a super-affectionate person now? No, but I am a lot warmer than I would have been if I had married a female version of me. I now reach for Holly's hand before she reaches for mine, and sometimes I hug her before she hugs me. That may not sound like I've made much progress, but I have.

 God, help me to show more affection for my spouse through physical touch.

REACH OUT AND TOUCH YOUR SPOUSE

Greet one another with a kiss of love.
—1 PET. 5:14

I'm a people watcher. I especially enjoy watching married couples and how they interact, though more than a few are painful to watch. These couples rarely talk unless about the kids or some decision that has to be made. Eye-contact and touching are minimal.

I love to see affectionate couples, like one couple at our church. They always walk arm-in-arm, talking in lively and involved tones. They clearly show their love for each other through their affectionate touching. It's quite a sight.

Holding hands is one of the ways Chris and I communicate our affection for each other. We have worked hard over the years to improve our communication and to display our love for each other like this. It is nice to be enjoying the fruits of that work. And, someday, we hope to be like that couple at church.

▼ *Lord, in simple ways, help me be vulnerable in my marriage and reach out to my spouse with a loving touch.*

AFFECTIONATE TOUCH HELPS INCREASE SEXUAL DESIRE

You have made my heart beat faster with a single glance of your eyes.   —SONG 4:9

Sarah and Andy had a common struggle. Andy portrayed Sarah as being sexually "frigid," and Sarah accused Andy of being a sex maniac! What started out as enjoyable sexual intimacy had now become a battleground. After dealing with pent-up resentments and fears, Sarah made an insightful observation: "It seems like the only time Andy touches me is when he wants sex!" We could now address this common issue by expanding their understanding of affectionate touch. A balanced relationship includes three kinds of touch.

Spiritual Touching: Holding hands to pray communicates spiritual agreement. Touch in church; embrace each other at times of great joy; hold hands as a family at the dinner prayer.

Soul Touching: Embrace each other as you depart and as you reunite. Go for a walk holding hands; walk arm in arm through the mall; sit close in the car; "claim" each other through embrace when you're in public!

Sexual Touching: Soft touching is usually preferred over grabbing or mauling. Kiss brushing of neck, back, or hand is often appropriate. Try body massage with lotion or baby oil. Fabrics can accentuate touch, so try silk sheets or nightwear.

▼ *Might the testimony of our sexual enjoyment be an example of God's plan for two becoming one flesh.*

APPRECIATION—GRATITUDE IN WORDS AND FEELINGS

Now I praise you, brethren, that you remember me.
—1 COR. 11:2

*W*hen I say "Thank you," I'm saying that I've noticed something you did for me, and that I care. Expressing appreciation also makes me vulnerable: I'm revealing the things that matter to me. But this is why saying thank you is such a powerful tool in developing close relationships. If you didn't matter to me, I wouldn't appreciate you so deeply—my saying so lets you know.

Many couples I see in counseling have trouble seeing each other in this light. Their focus tends to be on the negative: what *I* don't like; what *I* don't have; what *you* don't do. I challenge couples to "think appreciatively." There were enough positive things to bring them together—most couples were not forced down the marriage aisle! Thoughts of this first love often spark gratitude and new hope.

▼ *Father, remind me often of my partner's strengths . . . remind me of our first love.*

APPRECIATION FROM ABOVE

"This is My beloved Son, in whom I am well pleased."
                                                    —MATT. 3:17

*I*n this passage, the heavenly Father brags on His Son. The word *beloved* shows just how deep the sentiment goes. The Father's initiative here is also important—the Son didn't have to extract the comment. Fishing for compliments is futile, even if I receive them; heartfelt appreciation is what I really need.

Such a public display of appreciation may make you feel uncomfortable at first, but your spouse would benefit greatly. In counseling, I've given many a husband this simple—if scary—assignment: Next time you and your wife are with her parents, simply say, "I'm sure you already know this, but you have a very special daughter, and I'm glad she's my wife!"

▼ *Help me to let the world know how grateful I am for the partner You have given me.*

OPPOSITES ATTRACT

Fulfill my joy by being like-minded, having the same love, being of one accord, of one mind.
—PHIL. 2:2

$\mathcal{D}$avid and I are opposite in almost every way. He is laid-back, easy-going, an "I'll deal with it later" type. I'm compulsive, a "let's deal with it now, whip-and-drive" person. I couldn't see David's personality traits as positive; in fact, they used to drive me crazy!

Our opposite natures really surfaced when it came time to discipline the kids. David's approach of "just talk to them" was producing rebellion in me. My way of "nip it in the bud and don't spare the rod" was producing rebellion in the kids. We had to find a way to balance love and limits.

My greatest fear was that David wasn't involved enough. David saw his passiveness with the kids as a way to balance what he felt was my severity. There is a place for both approaches, but first we had to learn to trust God—with each other and with our kids.

Now I appreciate David's nature; I need his laid-back, easy-going ways to balance my compulsiveness.

▼ *I am grateful, Father, for Your wisdom and divine plan in giving me a spouse who complements me.*

APPRECIATION . . . EVEN FOR IRRITATIONS!

And we know that all things work together
for good to those who love God.
—ROM. 8:28

*W*hy do opposites attract one another?" That question is raised often by frustrated couples who feel "repelled" by all their differences. I felt that way myself, for years into our marriage. Teresa seemed so rigid. "Nip it in the bud, now" was her motto, while mine was "When in doubt—don't." At the first sign of my procrastination, her diligence was on me like a bulldog. I remember thinking, "God, why do I have a wife like this?"

Over time I came to see the answer. God knew I needed a wife just like Teresa. Although her diligence irritated and frustrated me, I could see clearly that my procrastination and passive resistance were weaknesses. God used her strengths to convict and change me. God's not finished with me yet . . . but what I once saw as a thorn in my flesh I now appreciate as a vital part of God's plan.

 Thank You, God, for knowing my needs and giving me a spouse who strengthens my weaknesses.

"THANKS, I APPRECIATE THAT!"

Her children rise up and call her blessed;
her husband also, and he praises her.
—PROV. 31:28

$\mathcal{W}$e all want appreciation. This is especially true in marriage, whether it's for dumping the garbage, taking the kids to soccer practice, or letting Aunt Mabel come visit.

I forget that sometimes. Coming home from a long day at work, preoccupied with my concerns and worries, I may overlook all the things Holly did that day to keep the Thurman family running smoothly, or give only a cursory "Thanks." Sometimes I don't even see the hurt and disappointment in Holly's eyes.

The flip side can be pretty powerful, though. On the days when I really let Holly know that I not only notice but greatly appreciate all she has done, her spirits lift, her step quickens, and her eyes get that sparkle back.

Appreciation—we all want it, we all sure need it, but we don't always offer it. It only takes a minute to tell your spouse why you appreciate who she is and what he does. Be specific. Then be on the lookout for that step to quicken and those eyes to sparkle!

 God, help me to be sensitive to my spouse's efforts,
and to praise them daily.

YOU'RE THE BEST THING THAT EVER HAPPENED TO ME

Let us have grace, by which we may serve God acceptably with reverence and godly fear.
—HEB. 12:28

$\int$oon after moving, we met a very nice couple who were also new in town. We hit it off immediately—our personalities and situations were so similar. After seeing them regularly at church, we missed them one Sunday morning: The husband, Sam, had had a massive heart attack.

It started me thinking—what if something like that happened to my own husband? It's so easy to forget how fragile life is and to take one's spouse for granted.

Right then and there, I wrote down all the things I appreciated about my husband, from sitting with the kids so I can nap, to wisely managing our finances—the list was long. I gave it to him, saying, "I just want you to know how much I love you and how much you mean to me and this family." He beamed from ear to ear!

We all need recognition and thanks for who we are and what we do. When was the last time you told your spouse what you value about him or her? Make a list today, and present it before you go to bed. It will mean the world!

 Lord, help me to convey to my spouse how grateful I am.

APPRECIATION NOTED IN A JOURNAL OF GRATEFULNESS

What shall I render to the LORD
For all His benefits toward me?
—PS. 116:12

*D*uring a challenging family time several years back, the Fergusons began journaling in a "Blessing Book." Teresa found an attractive journal, which we used to enter individual and family "blessings." We entered the date, how we were blessed, and how we had expressed appreciation. This exercise helped us focus more on the positives than the negatives and brought us together with grateful hearts.

Now Teresa and I take time to share regularly in a "blessing search." Each of us names a way we've been blessed recently by the other or in general, and then we express our appreciation. We look for unique qualities in each other, challenging character qualities, often over-looked blessings of life—health, provision, creation—and specific answers to prayer. The appreciation we express with a simple thanks, a note, a gift, helps to seal in our hearts the reality of the blessing and also encourages others.

▼ *Take time today to consider how you've been blessed by each other. Then find a way to show your appreciation.*

APPROVAL—TO THINK AND SPEAK WELL OF

*For he who serves Christ in these things
is . . . approved by men.*   —ROM. 14:18

The need for approval is so great that many a young person has sought it from peers at too high a price, and many a marriage has been ruined as it was found outside the home. Men seem to have a particular need for the "cheerleading" of a sensitive wife. Approval can be spoken, or written in special love notes. It can be lovingly shared in private, or publicly expressed in the presence of children, family, or friends.

Couples often come to counseling picking at one another about little things: "She leaves her keys, shoes, makeup all over the house"; "He is glued to the TV from dusk till midnight." What usually underlies such attacks is a need for approval. Complaining about sloppiness may mean, "Haven't you noticed how well I rearranged the garage?" Complaining about TV watching may mean, "Come outside and see how well my flowers are doing!" Never doubt that communication is a major issue in marriage!

▼ *Father, open my eyes to my partner's need for approval.*

APPROVAL MOTIVATES

*Be diligent to present yourself approved
to God.* —2 TIM. 2:15

*I*n counseling, we often tell couples to prepare a list of things they're grateful for in each other, then hold hands, look one another in the eye, and say: "I'm deeply grateful for the way you _____; it really means a lot to me." You'll be amazed at how powerful approval really is.

Where the approval comes from is equally important. A stranger's approval doesn't mean nearly as much as a friend's. Approval from a boss or co-worker is not nearly as precious as that from a spouse. And then within each of us is a deeper longing for the approval of the Creator. I didn't always feel that way; but the growing knowledge and experience of His grace—His unwarranted favor in spite of my performance—has motivated me to please Him!

▼ *Heavenly Father, help me to see and approve my spouse as You see and approve me.*

APPROVAL

Give, and it will be given to you.
—LUKE 6:38

*I*n my years as a counselor, I've met many women who have never gotten their husband's approval. They have felt criticized for their size, the way they dress, how they keep house, or how they cook. It hurts terribly to be condemned by the one person you want most to accept you—your spouse. A man can feel the same way if all he hears from his wife is what he's doing wrong.

David has set the standard in our family. He never puts me down, criticizes me, or picks over my faults. And that can be contagious! The more David honors me by showing his approval, the more I've wanted to do the same for him.

▼ *Father, thank You for giving Your approval so we can give to others.*

APPROVAL

All wives will honor their husbands, both
great and small. —EST. 1:20

$\mathcal{D}$ad was a Marine drill instructor, and approval was scarce when I was growing up. There were bed inspections to confirm the tightness of the sheets, but the words "I'm proud of you" were hard to come by.

I know now that I married Teresa hoping for her approval, expecting, in fact, that she would make up for all I had missed. At first when it didn't come, I tried harder to gain it. But that effort was followed by anger and then withdrawal when I still didn't get what I needed. I was on a vicious treadmill of "never enough," and the more I tried, performed, or bought, the worse things got.

Finally, fifteen years into marriage, during one of our "after-argument" talks, I put my finger on what was missing. I talked openly about how sad I felt, especially as a child longing to hear those words of praise and approval. Teresa comforted me, and a wonderful healing began as I sensed her understanding and comfort. A miracle began in her, too, freeing her to give approval and making her more sensitive as to when I might need it.

▼ *Might You, Father, through this marriage, restore years the locusts have eaten.*

TO APPROVE OR NOT TO APPROVE

Be diligent to present yourself approved
to God.
—2 TIM. 2:15

*M*y dad was an officer in the Air Force for over thirty years. During that time, he received numerous commendation medals for action above and beyond the call of duty. By the time he retired, his uniform had so many ribbons and medals on it it looked like a flower garden.

Obviously the Air Force approved of my dad, and they gave him medals to let him know. He must have felt proud to wear that uniform—I know I would have.

We have a chance to decorate our spouse's uniform every day, by offering "commendation medals" for service to a great cause—our marriage.

My dad worked hard to give the military his best, and he received a lot of approval for it. Our spouses often work just as hard to make marriage loving and enjoyable. They need our commendations as well.

If your spouse had a medal for every word of your approval, how full of medals would the uniform be?

▼ *God, please help me cover my spouse's uniform with medals of approval.*

SAFE AT HOME

*Be diligent to present yourself approved
to God.* —2 TIM. 2:15

I went to a society function last week, one of those that only rich, thin, and perfectly coiffured women attend. Gatherings like that always bring out the worst in me. I feel badly dressed, tongue-tied, and sorely in need of a dye job (I think I was one of only two brunettes in the whole place). On the surface everyone smiled and said hello, but I could tell they didn't really care.

We've all been in situations where we felt the odd man out, where everyone seems to know everyone else but you. And worse yet, you don't seem to be someone they *want* to know.

During that society function, all I could think of was home, where Chris was. It was comforting to know that when I walked in the front door I would be greeted by someone who gave me his loving approval no matter how I look or what I say or who I know. Marriage is supposed to be like that—no matter what you run into on the outside you have the approval you need when you get back home.

▼ *God, thank You that I am approved by You, and thank You for the approval my spouse gives me. Help me to return the favor whenever possible.*

APPROVAL THROUGH SHARING THANKS

I . . . do not cease to give thanks for you.
—EPH. 1:16

*W*e often remind couples in counseling that at one point in the relationship they saw enough positive things in each other to marry! Helping couples focus again on finding and expressing gratefulness is a key element in moving toward a more intimate marriage.

Begin sharing your thanks for each other this week by listing six areas of genuine thanks you have about this relationship. (Be specific, looking particularly for things you may have come to take for granted.) Then commit to practicing praise—not nagging—for the next week. Agree not to complain. Make a consistent effort to share praise from your "Thanks List," as well as at other times. Look for opportunities to share praise and appreciation privately, during daily conversations and private times, publicly, when in the company of others— family members, children, or friends—creatively, with special notes, cards, or gifts.

 Father, set a guard on my lips so that only words that build up might come forth.

ATTENTION—ENTERING ANOTHER'S "WORLD"

> *The members should have the same care one*
> *for another.* —1 COR. 12:25

*D*oes anyone really care about me? Am I important to anyone? Such questions express the universal need for attention.

Will anyone notice that I'm here or take initiative and enter into my world? The disciples may miss the importance of this need, but not the Messiah. He'll notice! He'll take initiative and move toward me! He'll enter into my world and meet me where I am! He'll communicate this interest in me even though others may not!

Christ's journey from Heaven to a manger in Bethlehem is the model for me in daily life: He left His world and entered mine. My world may be one of appointments, consultations, and phone calls, but I must leave it to enter Teresa's world of outdoor projects, socializing, and family fun. I've discovered that, as I do so, we share a deepened sense of oneness, a warmth of friendship, and a tenderness sparked by her gratitude.

▼ *Thanks, Jesus, for leaving Your world and entering mine because You loved me; might I do likewise for those I love.*

CHRIST GAVE ME ATTENTION

*And being found in appearance as a man,
He humbled Himself.*
—PHIL. 2:8

*C*hrist took the initiative and entered my world. That affirms my significance and declares my worth, not my accomplishments or my performance. God heeded my needs and moved toward me. He conveyed His loving interest in me by declaring me worthy of His only Son.

Among husbands and wives, as so often happens, each longs for attention from the other. We try to teach couples to express their needs and their approval rather than focus on the other's behavior. A wife who complains, "You've worked every night this week and I'm sick of it," is really saying, "I know how hard you've been working, but at the same time I am so lonely! I miss you." Compare the two statements. Which would you rather hear? Entering your partner's world can be a challenge, but the payoffs are great.

▼ *Lord, sensitize me to opportunities for conveying my loving interest in my partner.*

ENTER MY WORLD

In this the love of God was manifested toward us, that God has sent His only begotten Son into the world, that we might live through Him.   —1 JOHN 4:9

$\mathcal{I}$ love to be out in my yard. I love to mow, plant flowers, even pull weeds. I wanted David to share my pleasure. When I first asked him to join me, he refused. He thought I only wanted him to work! My feelings were hurt until I understood that my real need was for his attention.

As I was growing up, my family would always go outside in the evening. Mom would work puzzles, Dad watered the yard, and all the kids would play. Those times were special—that was when I had Mom and Dad's complete attention. Understanding this helped me see that David could spend time with me in other ways, and helped David understand my needs.

Now we both love being outside; I can putter and he can write or read because my real need is to be close to him. As the years go by, what we're doing seems less important than just being together.

▼ *Father, thank You for showing me how to enter the world of those I love best.*

ATTENTION—SHOWING INTEREST

The first man was of the earth, made of dust;
the second Man is the LORD from heaven.
—1 COR. 15:47

*T*hree-year-old Jason's temper tantrums were becoming extreme—he was banging his head and kicking holes in walls—and his father, Doug, brought him to me for assessment. It didn't take long to see the problem from my chair in our observation room.

When Doug entered the playroom, he noticed a Velcro dart board on the wall and began throwing the darts while Jason retrieved them for him. This lasted three or four minutes, until Jason noticed a Ninja Turtle play set on the floor. "Daddy, Daddy, let's play on the floor with Leonardo," Jason asked excitedly over and over again. Doug refused, saying, "You can play Turtles at home." As Jason's temper began to rise, his face flushed and his fists clenched. At his wits' end, Doug pleaded, "Don't cry, don't get mad. Forget about it now, and Saturday I'll take you to a University of Texas basketball game!" Jason relaxed and Doug escaped further embarrassment, but nowhere in our session had Doug really showed an interest in his son's world. Jason's world was not darts or basketball games; it was on the floor with the Turtles and his Dad's undivided attention.

▼ *Heavenly Father, help me leave the security of my own interests, as Christ did, and enter into my partner's enjoyment—with joy.*

MISSING THE FOREST FOR THE TREES

Pleasant words are like a honeycomb,
sweetness to the soul and health to the bones.
—PROV. 16:24

*H*ave you ever missed the forest for the trees in your marriage? You know what I mean—complaining about your partner's late hours while forgetting how that pays the bills, or seeing the things around the house that weren't done that day, while forgetting all the chores that were completed.

It's easy to focus on details and lose sight of the big picture. But for a marriage, this is deadly. If you don't work on that "big picture" view, the details can overwhelm you both.

Do you have a "big picture" view of your spouse? Do you consider the whole person when focusing on some point of weakness? Do you consider all of your partner's actions when you focus on what should or shouldn't have been done? Do you consider all of your partner's words when listening to something that is tough to hear?

The next time your spouse is late, or fails to fulfill a promise, or isn't responding to your needs the way you would like, try to take an honest look at the big picture before you react. It could make all the difference!

 God, help me, in my marriage, to see the whole picture, not just the things I don't like.

ALL EYES ARE ON YOU

LORD, what is man, that You take knowledge of Him?
—PS. 144:3

*O*ur son Matthew was irritable and restless. He complained he was bored, and picked on his sister more than usual. After a little probing, we discovered that all Matthew really wanted was more attention from Mom and Dad, some uninterrupted time when our eyes and ears were only for him. Helping him recognize his needs encouraged him to ask directly for our attention—an important step in maturity.

We husbands and wives want and need our spouse's attention too, but sometimes we don't get it. So instead of asking directly for attention, we start picking on each other like children, eliciting "negative" attention rather than the healthy kind.

It's so easy to fall into a pattern of not giving each other enough attention, isn't it? And it's easy to react childishly when we don't get the attention we want. Chris and I learned to set aside some time just for us each week that is quiet and unhurried so we can catch up with each other's lives. We both look forward to giving each other our full attention, and end up understanding each other better!

If you need a "two-way street" time for giving and receiving attention, try asking directly, then set aside the time you need to make sure it happens.

▼ *God, help us have the kind of marriage You intended for us, and the attention we need from each other.*

WEEKLY ATTENTION AT MARRIAGE STAFF MEETINGS

I will seek the one I love.
—SONG 3:2

*I*n addition to our periodic counseling sessions, we have couples commit to a weekly "Marriage Staff Meeting" where they'll complete their counseling homework and begin the lifelong discipline of investing in the relationship.

Developing and maintaining marital intimacy requires a consistent investment in quality sharing. Our intimacy increased when we began to schedule a weekly time together. We don't leave this to chance! Lunch on Thursday; Tuesday night after the children are asleep; Saturday morning breakfast. We make our time together a priority—we make it inviolate, as much as possible. The consistency each week is important, but the emotional benefit of prioritizing each other in this time encourages our closeness. And we protect the time from interruptions and distractions by getting away from the office to a "quiet" place at home. As you're planning your next week, make time to be together. A fearful thought for many couples may be *What in the world would we talk about?* A typical agenda might include calendar coordination, family goals, parenting plans, just listening to each other, or sharing appreciation.

▼ *Lord, remind me of the need to consistently invest time with the most important people in my life—You and my spouse.*

CARE—PROVIDING FOR ANOTHER'S NEED

*So he went to him and bandaged his wounds
. . . brought him to an inn, and took care
of him.*
—LUKE 10:34

The good Samaritan looked beyond himself and saw another's need. This selfless attitude is the essence of what God did for me: Though I was still in sin, He selflessly gave His Son. His provision is exactly what I needed—forgiveness, acceptance, love, purpose in life. Without selfish preoccupations, I can, like the good Samaritan, become sensitive to the genuine needs of another. I can *care!*

It's sobering to think that I hold within me the "provisions" that Teresa needs: acceptance, security, and comfort. To share these blessings with her is to care for her. I can overcome any selfish preoccupations by being mindful that these blessings are from God. When I'm not preoccupied with me but with Him, He often prompts me to consider Teresa!

▼ *Lord, I'm grateful for Your selfless example and for showing me how my partner and I can care for each other.*

CONCERNED ENOUGH TO CARE

The Son of Man has come to seek and to save.
                                                    —LUKE 19:10

Christ is the ultimate good Samaritan—He cares for the uncared about; He is concerned for the unnoticed. I'm so glad Christ didn't pass by on the other side of the road as I lay there in helpless, hopeless pain. I'm so glad He didn't just shout, "Take care of it yourself," or "Sorry, can't stop now. I'm in a hurry." I am sad when I think of the times I've given that message to people around me, either with words or by neglect.

Leaving my side of the road to come to yours is what caring is all about. For too many years I didn't participate enough in caring for our children. From my selfish and biased perspective, I viewed raising the children as Teresa's "side of the road." Secure and uninvolved on "my" side, I was ready enough to bark orders or criticize Teresa's parenting. Through pain and stress, God began to get my attention and change my attitude. Slowly I began to join Teresa in parenting *our* children.

▼ *Heavenly Father, keep me attuned to opportunities for stopping on Life's road, and caring for all who might need me.*

COLD REFRIGERATORS

What is man that You are mindful of him,
And the son of man that You visit him?
—PS. 8:4

$\mathcal{D}$avid never takes time during the day for food. I was so concerned about this that I bought him a small refrigerator for his office. I even went out of my way to keep it stocked. I was very proud of myself, but that quickly turned to frustration: he didn't even stop to take anything from it! Only when I put juice and a muffin in his message box would he eat during the day.

I finally understood that that cold, impersonal refrigerator couldn't give him the attention he needed. Only when I got personally involved did he feel cared for.

▼ *God, You are a Father who cares deeply about our every need.*

CARE IN THE LITTLE THINGS

Her husband is known in the gates, When he sits among the elders of the land.
—PROV. 31:23

I had just completed six hours of back-to-back counseling sessions following an early morning meeting, and was squeezing in return phone calls along the way. An afternoon of three more sessions stretched before me, with nothing to look forward to but a long drive home after dark.

Paul warned the Galatians, "Let us not grow weary while doing good," but weariness had set it. As I rushed past my message box—checking for more phone calls— I was greeted instead by manna from heaven, in the form of a soft drink, my favorite crackers, and a short love note! Teresa had passed through the office and thought of me.

My whole perspective changed: "I've been thought of! I'm important! I'm loved!" Her initiative and sensitivity spoke volumes. As I walked back toward my office, I told everyone who would listen just how I had been cared for by someone who loved me!

▼ *Thank You, Father, for the simplicity of caring.*

CARING ENOUGH TO LOVINGLY GIVE

*But we were gentle among you, just as a
nursing mother cherishes her own children.*
—1 THESS. 2:7

$\mathcal{I}$ was an avid tennis player in my teens and twenties. I couldn't get enough of the sport and would play every day, for two or three hours if I could.

Of course, an avid tennis player had to *look* like one, which meant having the right clothes. One sporting goods company made warm-ups that were considered the best. They were made out of a silky nylon, and were pretty expensive, especially for someone in graduate school. I wanted a pair of those warm-ups so badly I could taste it, and envied my tennis buddies who could afford them. But Holly and I were married about that time, and they were simply beyond our budget.

Our first Christmas together arrived. We opened the presents we had bought for each other, and guess what I got? That's right—those warm-ups. Holly knew how much they meant to me. I wore them to bed that night, and I have been wearing them ever since, eleven years later.

What's the big deal about a pair of tennis warm-ups, you ask? Well, the big deal is that Holly cared enough to listen to the desires of my heart, and meet them, no matter how small or insignificant. Those warm-ups were her way of saying that what mattered to me mattered to her, and I plan to keep them until they fall apart.

▼ *God, help me care deeply about the things my spouse cares about.*

WITHOUT BEING ASKED

He knows those who trust in Him.
—NAH. 1:7

*W*hat makes you feel cared about? I feel cared about most when Chris does something unexpected, like come home early from work to babysit so I can run errands, or do the wash when it was my turn, or surprise me with an invitation to lunch just because he was thinking about me and wanted to spend time together.

Chris feels cared about when I anticipate his needs and do kind things without being asked. It shows him that I really care. Sometimes I watch the kids so he can sleep late on Saturday, or bring him an ice-cold glass of his favorite drink when he's mowing the lawn. I think he especially likes that hug at the end of the day, when I run out to greet him before he's out of the car.

It feels good when someone cares enough to know what makes us happy and does it without being asked. What would make your spouse feel cared about? What could you do, without being asked, that would let him or her know you really, deeply care?

▼ *Dear Lord, help us to know our spouse's needs, and to meet them without being asked.*

LOVE NOTES SAY I CARE!

How beautiful is your love . . . my bride!
How much better is your love than wine.
—SONG 4:10 NASB

$\mathcal{W}$hy write to someone I live with? Such is the questioning of the overly logical and rational mind—but such questioning kills romance!

It's the little reminders that warm the heart because they say "I was thinking of you"; "You are important to me"; "I went out of my way to find a card"; "I trust you with my heart—to value my vulnerable expressions of love." Finding "I'll be thinking of you" in a coat pocket, purse, or lunch box can bring joy to your spouse guaranteed to last all day. An "I love you" note on a mirror, car seat, or countertop brings a pleasant sensation that can carry over until you meet again.

Why not, this week, go out of your way to creatively communicate "I love you"?

▼ *Remind me often of the beauty of my partner's love and help me express the wonder of my gratefulness.*

COMFORT—TO CONSOLE WITH A TENDER WORD OR TOUCH

Therefore comfort one another with these words. —1 THESS. 4:18

*C*are" for someone is usually expressed by concrete actions. "Comfort" is less tangible. It is an expression of the heart, saying, "It saddens me to see you hurting, because I love you." Reassuring words are often accompanied by a tender touch. By sharing my feelings for you during a time of hurt or loss, I become vulnerable, too.

Isn't it wonderful that the Bible portrays Jesus as caring and emotional! Like us, He experiences joy and grief, excitement and compassion! (John 17:13; Mark 3:5; Luke 10:21; Matt. 14:14) What a contrast to the worldly pressures for detached performance, and perfection at all costs. Empathy with another's pain originates in this realm of feelings. From the depth of these feelings, comfort rises up and blesses others.

 Thank You, Heavenly Father, for the comfort of Your holy Word.

THE MYSTERY OF COMFORT

Blessed be the God . . . of all comfort, who comforts us . . . that we may be able to comfort others. —2 COR. 1:3–4

*C*omfort can't be given from a distance, so Christ left Heaven and became as one of us. Comfort is *not* giving advice; Christ felt the pain of rejection, betrayal, and loss so that He might empathize with hurting people. Comfort doesn't come in profound proclamations, but in quiet reassurance. What an example He's been of how I might share the comfort I've received with others.

I can recall being unbelievably insensitive in the early years of our marriage. If at the end of a long day I found Teresa sad or even tearful about one of life's inevitable daily hurts, I might say, "What's wrong with you *now?*" (blaming). "Well, next time maybe you can handle it differently" (giving advice). "This is a great homecoming! I should have stayed at work" (being a martyr). None sound very comforting! After several years of this, I began to ask myself: "What does *God* feel for Teresa in her pain?" The answer was clear: *He feels sadness for her; He hurts for her. Maybe,* I thought, *it's O.K. for me to feel sad and hurt for her, too. Maybe what she needs is just for me to say, "I can see that you're really upset and I hurt for you because I love you."*

▼ *Father, draw me close for Your comfort, then bring me close to share it.*

FEBRUARY 21

SHARE HUGS, NOT JUST ADVICE

And look! The tears of the oppressed, But they have no comforter. —ECCL. 4:1

$\mathcal{D}$arla, one of my clients, was telling me how hurt she was by the breakup with her boyfriend; how badly he had treated her, and yet how she really wanted to be with him. When I asked if she had a close friend to share her hurt with, or a family member she could confide in, Darla sighed. "All I get is advice—and some of the advice hurts more than the breakup! Advice like 'Just dump him' and 'Don't you dare crawl back to him.'" I touched her as I told her gently how sorry I was that her friends didn't understand her pain or her need to be listened to.

Darla hugged me on the way out. What she needed more than advice was to be comforted, and, tragically, comfort is rarely given between adults. Merely to listen and touch someone while we're talking seems too simple, but often that's all anyone really needs.

 Father, You gave first to me so I can give to others. Thanks, Father, for the power of the comforting word or touch.

COMFORT IS NOT ADVICE

But I fear, lest somehow . . . your minds may
be corrupted from the simplicity that is in
Christ.
—2 COR. 11:3

*W*hy is it that when Teresa is sharing her disappointment or hurt, I find it so difficult to genuinely comfort her? In giving comfort, there's a subtle simplicity that is easy to overlook.

I usually respond in one of two ways: If I've contributed to Teresa's hurt or disappointment, I tend to react defensively. Only by opening myself to the Spirit can I look beyond myself and truly comfort her.

If I haven't contributed to Teresa's hurt or disappointment, I react by giving advice: "Maybe next time you might try . . ." On reflection, I've come to realize that giving advice is just a reflex prompted by my fears of inadequacy—fear that I won't know what to do or how to fix it, whatever "it" is. But the solution is the same—allow the Spirit's control to look beyond myself and truly comfort another.

▼ *Today let me walk in the Spirit rather than seek to*
fulfill my own desires.

LEARNING TO WALK

But I would strengthen you with my mouth,
And the comfort of my lips would relieve
your grief.   **—JOB 16:5**

Our daughter, Kelly, recently learned to walk. It was fun watching her as she went through the various stages of crawling, pulling up, standing, taking a step and falling (thank goodness our bottoms are padded when we are babies), and then walking around to her heart's content. During that process, she took some nasty falls and needed us to comfort her.

Learning to be intimate in marriage has some striking parallels. When we first marry, we are emotional babies, immature in our ability to really love each other. As we grow in marriage, standing up and taking a few steps of true, sacrificial love becomes easier. Ultimately, if we work hard enough at it, we learn to walk in love. Throughout that whole process, we are going to make some pretty bad mistakes. Those are the moments when we need to comfort each other.

My daughter has learned to walk fairly well for a one year old, and it is a joy to see. In my ability to love my wife, I am still crawling most of the time. But with God's help, and only with His help, I hope to walk steadily someday. Before I die, I want to be running! What a joy it must be to God when He sees us go from crawlers to walkers to runners in love.

▼ *God, help us to comfort each other when we fall in our efforts to love.*

THE BITTER WITH THE SWEET

Pleasant words are like a honeycomb,
Sweetness to the soul and health to the bones.
—PROV. 16:24

On and off for a week, an excruciating pain had been shooting through my lower abdomen. Visits to my doctor and even one to the emergency room had not yielded any definite answers. Was I pregnant? Some tests came back positive, some negative. Had I miscarried? That afternoon, while I was in my doctor's office, I had another painful attack. He told me to make arrangements for my kids and call my husband because I was going in for immediate surgery. I had a tubal pregnancy.

My husband and children rushed down to the hospital. When I awoke from surgery, Chris was alongside me, wiping my forehead. Just seeing him was such a comfort! He held my hand and told me the doctor said I would be fine. Later in my hospital room we sat together and went over all that had happened. I was quite upset and still in pain, but Chris was right there, tenderly consoling me. God used him, as He often does, to comfort me in a bumpy time.

We all need comfort during the tough times. In marriage, comfort from a spouse can mean the difference between a crisis that overwhelms us and a crisis we overcome.

▼ *Thank You, God, for Your love, which comforts us in our sorrows. Help us to regularly give and receive comfort in our marriage.*

COMFORT WITH EMOTIONAL RESPONDING

*The Spirit of the Lord God is
upon Me . . .
To comfort all who mourn.*
—ISA. 61:1–2

*L*ori tearfully described her disappointment over Sam totally forgetting her birthday. As Lori sat next to him on the couch, hurting deeply over her felt rejection, Sam finally responded: "I had such a busy week, and the kids' schedules kept us out every night. I'll make it up to you." While Sam's comments were all true, they didn't help Lori's pain one bit.

When emotion is shared, logic, reasons, and facts don't help. Emotional hurt is not healed with explanations, criticism, or reminders of "my hurt." Emotional openness needs to be reciprocated with emotion. As a vocabulary of emotions is developed by each spouse, the next step is to learn to answer emotion with emotion.

After exploring his feelings about his wife's pain, Sam was able to communicate a more comforting message: "Lori, I can really see that you're hurting, and I genuinely regret my part in hurting you. I deeply care about you and love you. Will you forgive me?"

Lori was able to receive Sam's confession and comfort, freeing them to enjoy each other. Give particular attention this week to increasing your level of emotional responding. Facts, logic, and reasons don't comfort— share more emotion!

▼ *Teach me, Father, of Your comforting ways.*

COMPASSION—TO SUFFER WITH ANOTHER

"I have compassion on the multitude."
—MATT. 15:32

*C*hrist had compassion on the tired and hungry multitude because they had a need. His compassion was based not on their performance but on their pain. He could identify with them, for He had experienced forty days in the wilderness without food. Compassion is the caring response to another's need and pain. I can't multiply bread and fish, but I *can* show my concern.

When Christ felt compassion, He acted. He instructed the disciples to organize the crowd. A lad's lunch was secured, prayer offered, and the multitudes fed. When caring actions are few and far between, compassion is lacking. When insensitivity is commonplace, compassion is needed. Compassion is the divine power compelling us to act. When my compassion ebbs, I recall Christ's compassion for me. He left Heaven—just for me! Moved by compassion, He walked up Calvary's hill—just for me!

▼ *Father, remind me often of Your compassion toward me.*

GOD'S ENDLESS COMPASSION

He will again have compassion on us.
—MIC. 7:19

*M*y compassion tends to run out, but God's never will. He will *again* have compassion on me. The thought comes to mind, "It's *my* turn to receive compassion. I'm tired of giving!" God never thinks that. Genuine compassion focuses not on one's own need but upon another's pain: If you hurt, I hurt for you! If you weep, I weep with you. If you rejoice, I rejoice. We meet one another at the point of suffering or joy and walk through it together.

A special friend at the clinic where Teresa and I work speaks often of our need for a "journey-mate," someone to walk with through life's inevitable mountaintops and valleys. We've learned that parents can be this for their children—not a coach barking orders or a passive observer, but a *journey-mate*. We try to play this role for each other, as we walk through the excitement and heartache, joy and disappointment of our life together.

▼ *Make us, Father, journey-mates in our walk through life.*

IT'S ALL RIGHT

The Lord is very compassionate and merciful.
—JAMES 5:11

*W*e were eating in an Atlanta coffee shop when I discovered I'd lost the $50 bill we were going to use to pay our restaurant bill. I panicked when I realized the money was gone and began berating myself. David was so gentle and compassionate. "We can pay our bill," he reassured me. "Everything is all right."

What a contrast to another incident, when I was a young girl! Mother had given me money to go to the store to buy supplies for a Girl Scout outing. Somewhere along the way, I lost the money. I felt so bad coming home empty-handed, and instead of compassion and understanding, I was sternly sent back to find it. I'll never forget how all alone and fearful I felt when I couldn't find that money. As a child then and as an adult now, I need someone to understand my hurt and to feel compassion toward me, to reassure me that everything will be all right.

▼ *Father, thank You for understanding my hurts and giving me compassion when I need it.*

COMPASSION FOLLOWS FROM COMFORT

And when Jesus went out He saw a great multitude: and He was moved with compassion for them.　　—MATT. 14:14

*C*ompassion seems to spring from gratitude for comfort received. On hearing of the beheading of John the Baptist, Christ withdrew onto the Sea of Galilee. He didn't pretend the tragic news didn't bother Him, He didn't minimize His grief. He simply allowed His Father to comfort Him. Compassion for the assembled multitudes followed.

Sandy brought her husband, Richard, to counseling after twelve years of marriage, complaining that though she *knew* he loved her, she didn't often *feel* his love. Richard was a classic case of the macho man taught to minimize his own pain. In fact, when his mom died five years earlier, he had never really mourned her death, even though they had been very close. Focusing on Richard's needs rather than his shortcomings, I told Sandy to tell him how sad she felt over his loss and the loneliness he must feel. I left the room as Sandy held his hand and compassionately poured out her sorrow for him. Richard wept openly as years of pent-up grief flooded out. But there were also tears of joy—that someone cared about his hurt. Having received compassion, over the next few sessions Richard began to learn how to reciprocate.

▼ *God of all comfort, please comfort me that I may be able to comfort others.*

HOW'S YOUR PLIMSOLL MARK?

And be kind to one another, tenderhearted, forgiving.
                                        —EPH. 4:32

In 1876, the British government, led by Samuel Plimsoll, passed a law requiring ships to mark their bows. If the so-called Plimsoll mark went below the waterline, the ship was carrying too much cargo and some had to be removed.

Loving our spouse means watching for that "Plimsoll mark." You know what I mean. By the end of the day, has life's load pushed your partner below the physical, emotional, and spiritual waterline? If so, ask a few important questions: Is your burden too heavy? Can I do anything to lighten your load? What worries can we toss overboard to get your "Plimsoll mark" back above the waterline?

We need the same from them, but real love means looking out for our partner before we look out for ourselves. So the next time you meet your spouse at the doorway after a long day, check that "Plimsoll mark." Maybe you can help lighten the load.

▼ *God, help us be compassionate about the burdens we each bear and help us stay afloat when life is stormy.*

IN SICKNESS AND IN HEALTH

*I . . . will comfort them, And make them
rejoice rather than sorrow.*
—JER. 31:13

*M*y dad was diagnosed with cancer when I was 16,
and died at home four years later, on December 25. He
had tried surgery, chemotherapy, radiation, even mega-
doses of vitamins and special diets, anything that might
help. But nothing did. That time was very difficult for all
of us, especially for him. One minute he'd be up and
hopeful, and the next, deeply distressed and irritable.

The most memorable aspect of that time was the way
my mother handled herself. She rarely left his side. She
ran all his errands, bought and administered his medication, cooked his special meals, listened to him and
encouraged him. Even when his pain and frustration
made him difficult to deal with, she'd try her best to be
calm and patient. She stood by him—through it all—till
the end.

Compassion—we kids saw the word living and
breathing in the form of my mother. Because of her,
compassion, for each one of us, has a special touch,
look, and sound. And her example has enabled us to
draw closer to others who have experienced serious illness in their lives.

Thank you, Mom. I hope you realize what a beautiful
gift you gave to your children.

▼ *Lord, help me show the compassion my spouse needs
to face life's ups and downs.*

A COMPASSIONATE FRIEND

*Therefore, as the elect of God, . . . put on
tender mercies.*
—COL. 3:12

*H*urts, irritations, unmet needs—life is full of them.
How ironic that marriage often magnifies them! The
passing critical comment from a co-worker might be forgotten quickly, while the same offered by a family member might fester for days. If a casual friend shows a lack
of interest in our conversation, we probably think nothing of it; but if a spouse fails to give us undivided attention, look out! We might have great difficulty
remembering birthdays, anniversaries, or where the car
keys are, but we remember with incredible detail how
long it has been since we've had sex.

Why is my partner feeling this way? Is my spouse
over-reacting? Would I feel the same in an identical situation? Surprisingly, none of these questions are as important as simply caring about your partner's pain.
Instead, ask "How could I be more compassionate
toward you when you're upset, sad, or anxious?"

▼ *Help me, Father, extend Your compassion.*

CONFESSION—OPEN ACKNOWLEDGMENT OF WRONGS COMMITTED

Confess your trespasses to one another.
—JAMES 5:16

*T*here may be no greater "unlived" exhortation than this one. Ever since the Fall, the flesh wants to justify, rationalize, and blame. I struggle to ignore the log in my own eye, even as it becomes all too evident. But in doing so, great blessings go untapped.

Tremendous worth is communicated to another person by confessing, "Our relationship is so valuable! I don't want my mistakes to damage it."

Some of the most dramatic changes in counseling occur as a couple becomes willing to examine ways in which they've hurt each other. "Have I been rejecting? Disrespectful? Insensitive? Have I hurt you with selfishness, abusive language, or skewed priorities?" Then, each spends time alone with God, confessing (acknowledging) the wrong committed. What emerges is a godly sorrow, a heart broken by the sobering knowledge of Christ's death and God's forgiveness. Now grateful and contrite, each feels a divine urgency to seek the other's forgiveness.

▼ *Bring me often before You, Father, to acknowledge my wrongs; then send me, grateful and forgiven, to confess to my spouse.*

CONFESSION IS PAINFUL

He was wounded for our transgression, He was bruised for our iniquities.

—ISA. 53:5

*C*onfession is no doubt one of the most misunderstood biblical truths—and one of the most difficult to carry out. Many couples who come for counseling complaining of little love and much unresolved hurt don't practice genuine confession to each other. Many offer meaningless platitudes: "If I've hurt you, I'm sorry." Many use apology manipulatively, to blame the other: "I'm sorry I lost my temper but I just get tired of your complaining." And many never even try to apologize, thinking that time will make the hurt go away.

Confession is from two Greek words meaning "speak the same." If I have been selfish, critical, unloving, or disrespectful, I must first "speak together" with God (1 John 1:9) and then to my spouse (James 5:16). But I must be ready to accept the pain and sorrow of Christ's death for my sins—I've been a part of killing Him! Our hearts must first be broken so that the forgiving, healing ministry of marriage reconciliation can begin.

▼ *Grant me, O God, a clean heart, and then prompt me to make it right with my spouse.*

WRONG! WHO, ME?

*I acknowledged my sin to You, And my
iniquity I have not hidden.* —PS. 32:5

$\mathcal{D}$avid and I were in his office planning our evening. I
was going to pick him up after work and then meet our
son Eric and his girlfriend, Meleah, for dinner. David
said he'd be finished at 6:30. Well, from past experience, I just "knew" he would be late, so I told him I'd
be there around 7:00. When I left him at the office, I
was assuming he would be late. I didn't expect the best
from him. I needed to confess to him my attitude was
wrong.

Most of us don't like to confess our mistakes; most of
us don't even know how. But confession is simply agree-
ing with God that my actions, attitude, or behavior is not
in line with His plan for my life. I first confessed to God
and then to David that what I had said was wrong, then
I asked for forgiveness. Hurt is an inevitable part of
marriage, but confessing my wrongs keeps the lines of
communication and intimacy open.

▼ *God, confessing to You and to others keeps me in
right relationship with You.*

EXALTED BY CONFESSION

"He who humbles himself will be exalted."
—MATT. 23:12

There's no quicker path to humility than confession. Confession turns the searchlight of God's truth upon my wrongs. Having seen them, I openly declare them and seek forgiveness—first from God, then from others (like my spouse!). Harsh words, broken promises, or hurtful actions can all initiate confession. It seems to be most meaningful after a time of brokenness with the Lord.

Confession is also a powerful paradox. I've seen many a wife gain respect for the husband who confesses in brokenness his wrongs toward her, for from brokenness, strength of character appears. From admission of inadequacy, truthful, God-centered adequacy appears. Such vulnerability can be scary, but it can be rewarding, too. The exaltation of a humble and forgiven heart is priceless.

▼ *Thank You, Heavenly Father, for teaching me that when I am weak, then I am strong.*

LOVE MEANS NEVER HAVING TO SAY YOU ARE SORRY???

For I will declare my iniquity; I will be in anguish over my sin. —PS. 38:18

*R*emember the movie *Love Story* with Ali McGraw and Ryan O'Neal? Millions loved it. I thought it was one of the dumbest movies I had ever seen.

The most ludicrous line in the movie was, "Love means never having to say you're sorry." You've got to be kidding! Love, true love, means having to say we are sorry all the time! Why? Because we mess up all the time, and the only right thing to do is honestly acknowledge our error, ask for forgiveness, and dedicate ourselves to not doing it again. If we have to, we do this over and over.

So, forgive me if I think *Love Story* was unrealistic. "I'm sorry" are the two most important words we can say when we err. They are part of the humbling process that God uses to make us more mature, intimate partners.

Please keep telling your spouse you are sorry for all the wrongs you have done and that you are willing to do better. Don't buy the *Love Story* notion that saying "I'm sorry" somehow means you don't really love each other deeply enough.

▼ *God, please help us to confess wrongdoing to each other, ask for forgiveness, and truly dedicate ourselves to doing better.*

GOOD FOR THE SOUL

He who covers his sins will not prosper, but whoever confesses and forsakes them will have mercy.
                                        —PROV. 28:13

*A*shley, you are so weird!" I could hear my son's voice from the other room. "Matthew, please come here. You are not to talk to your sister like that again—do you understand?" "But Mom," he replied, "you don't always talk nice to Daddy."

Ouch! That hurt. I had been giving Matthew mixed messages—saying one thing with words and teaching another with my behavior. I could see now which one he had adopted!

I hadn't realized the impact of some unkind things I had said to Chris. Through my son, God showed me how hurtful I'd been to my husband. When I went to Chris, saying, "Honey, I'm sorry for treating you so unkindly," he hugged me and gladly offered his forgiveness.

Together we talked with the kids about what had happened. We wanted them to understand that it wasn't enough to know you had done something wrong. We tried to help them see that true sorrow means openly confessing the wrong done. Confession is good for the soul. We hope that becomes a habit in the Thurman family, and in your family, too.

▼ *God, help my spouse and me get into the habit of confessing our sins to one another so that our wrongs are out in the open and faced maturely.*

HOW TO HEAL THE MARRIAGE HURTS: CONFESSION AND FORGIVENESS

Purge me with hyssop, and I shall be clean;
Wash me, and I shall be whiter than snow.
—PS. 51:7

*H*urts don't simply go away. Time doesn't spontaneously heal resentments, and trying harder doesn't compensate for guilt. It's sobering to realize that selfishness, or an unloving attitude, or abusive words were exactly why Christ had to die for me.

Each of you take time alone to list ways in which you may have hurt your spouse or your marriage. Ask yourself, "Have I been selfish, critical or negative, insensitive, disrespectful, verbally abusive, unsupportive, unfaithful?" Then, confess to God and receive His forgiveness (1 John 1:9). (For example: God, I have deeply hurt You and my spouse by my _____. These are very wrong, and I ask You to forgive me. Please change me into the kind of person I need to be.)

Come back together and share your lists and request forgiveness (James 5:16). (For example: I've seen that I've hurt you deeply by being _____. I have been very wrong. Will you forgive me?)

▼ *Lord, break through my justifications and my own pain to help me see and then confess how I've hurt this special one.*

CONSIDERATION—TAKING INTO ACCOUNT ANOTHER'S IDEAS, FEELINGS, AND NEEDS

And Julius treated Paul kindly.
—ACTS 27:3

$\mathcal{D}$octor Luke tells us of the Apostle Paul's journey to Rome as a prisoner. At the port city of Sidon, Paul receives favorable treatment from a Roman official, Julius: he is allowed to "go to his friends and receive care." Paul's need for friendship and caring support was considered. Consideration is looking beyond someone's status and discerning the needs of a unique person.

Show your consideration by truly knowing your partner. I know Teresa well enough to buy flowers and not candy; I know the colors she likes, and the name of her favorite perfume and soap; I know she likes to socialize, but not stay out too late; prefers me to drive, but with caution; and likes doors opened for her. She likes to "people watch," shop, and drink coffee—but decaf after 5:00 P.M. I "consider" these things, all of which are a part of what makes Teresa, Teresa—and I love her.

▼ *Thank You, God, for my unique, special partner.*

CONSIDERATION REQUIRES SACRIFICE

"It is more blessed to give than to receive."
—ACTS 20:35

*L*ove is not real love without sacrifice, without giving of oneself. Our lives would be spiritually empty had not God given up his own Son for us.

But what of *our* sacrifices—what do they entail? To genuinely give consideration to another's ideas, feelings, and needs, I must be willing to sacrifice my own. Many's the time I've asked Teresa how she wants to spend a free afternoon, hoping all the while that we could do what *I* wanted—not exactly showing consideration, is it?

Focusing on another's needs requires sacrifice, but can also bring inexpressible joy. It gives God the opportunity to bring forth the greater blessing that comes from giving. Giving consideration does not mean that I can't have ideas, feelings, and needs of my own. But it is God who will look after me while I look after my spouse. God can be trusted to take what I have given, press it down, shake it together, and give back to me overflowing (Luke 6:38)!

▼ *Today, Lord, grant me an unusual openness to listen to my partner, to consider ideas, feelings, and needs, and to lovingly give of myself.*

HOME ALONE

*And let us consider one another in order to
stir up love and good works.*
—HEB. 10:24

$\mathcal{D}$avid was working on a doctorate degree from Oxford
and needed to spend a week in Tennessee. His plane
reservations required him to stay over the weekend, so
he flew me out to meet him. I looked forward to having
quality time with him, but a weekend away from home
was not my first choice.

You see, David and I travel quite a bit, especially on
weekends. For the last few years, I have spent almost
every weekend away from home. While most people regard a weekend away as a treat, the opposite is true for
me.

David's need for me, however, brought me more joy
than being at home alone. I'm grateful that he wants me
to share time with him. Making sacrifices for each other
gives us a sense of importance in our relationship.

▼ *Father, help me to always be considerate of my partner's needs.*

KEEP ME IN MIND!

Now to Him who is able to do exceedingly
abundantly above all we ask or think.
—EPH. 3:20

𝓔ven before I saw my need, God had already taken it into consideration. Long before I acknowledged my need for His Son, He had provided Him as my substitute. My heavenly Father has taken me into account in His plans for eternity. Even now, he is attentive to my need. Genuine consideration is just like that—it considers another's past and responds in accepting love; it makes provision for the future; and gives sensitive attention to the present. Taking into account another's needs or point of view—that's what God's love is all about.

It means a lot to me when Teresa takes note of an extra busy week and fills it with special and tender touches of love: a favorite meal after a long day, pampering me in my easy chair at home, or a comfortable embrace at bedtime. She's "considered" me and that feels great!

 Father, keep me looking beyond the routines to see the real needs.

CONSIDER THIS

Husbands, likewise, dwell with them with
understanding, giving honor to the wife.
—1 PET. 3:7

*H*ave you ever gone out on a double date with another married couple and humiliated your spouse by acting less than mature and loving? You know—overreacting to something in a way that embarrassed him. Or cutting her off all evening long just to make your opinions heard. Or just not behaving in a loving way.

Sometimes I am so concerned about whether or not the other couple is having a good time, I forget to be sensitive to Holly. I'm afraid that if the other couple isn't enjoying themselves, they won't like us or want to go out with us again. So I focus my attention on them, and Holly gets lost in the shuffle.

Holly isn't the kind of person to complain when that happens, but I know it hurts her. And with reason. That kind of behavior is a message that she isn't the most important person in my life, that the couple we are with is more important. This isn't what I really feel, but actions speak louder than words.

So whether you are on a double date, alone, or with the kids, do what I need to do: Let everyone know that your spouse's feelings and needs are of utmost importance to you. That is the kind of consideration we need to give to one another.

▼ *God, help me be considerate toward my spouse no matter who we are with or what situation we are in.*

YOU MATTER TO ME

*But in lowliness of mind, let each esteem
others better than himself.* —PHIL. 2:3

𝓔ven though Don professed to be a Christian, he told Kathy, his wife, he would not go to church. He didn't see the need for it and made it clear that he didn't want to be nagged. Every Sunday morning, Kathy would get up, fix breakfast, and dress herself and their three children, while Don sat reading the paper.

She was convinced that Don's problem stemmed from the fact that his parents dropped him off at the church door every Sunday but never set foot in there themselves. So, though she felt frustrated, she was determined to raise her kids in the church. Consistency was the key, she believed.

Don was impressed with Kathy's behavior. He admired her efforts to get herself and the kids ready for church, and often felt guilty as he watched her hurry around on Sunday mornings. She never complained or nagged. Although she disagreed with his wishes, she had been considerate of them.

One Sunday, Don jumped out of bed as the alarm went off and hurried to wake the kids. Kathy, in disbelief, asked, "Hey, what's going on?" Don replied, "Sweetheart, I want to help you because you are doing the right thing. We need to raise our kids in the church, and you have lovingly shown me how."

▼ *God, help us to show consideration to each other in all possible ways, especially through respecting each other's choices and leading by example.*

CONSIDER YOUR PARTNER'S NEEDS

"How much more will your Father who is in heaven give good things to those who ask Him!"
—MATT. 7:11

To help you get in touch with the type of "strokes" you and your spouse enjoy, check the items that appeal to your mate in Column 1 and to you in Column 2.

☐ ☐ Holding hands
☐ ☐ Going for a walk
☐ ☐ Being served a favorite meal
☐ ☐ Being told "I love you"
☐ ☐ Helping with the kids
☐ ☐ Being approached sexually

☐ ☐ Taking a shower together
☐ ☐ Getting a back rub or massage
☐ ☐ Being praised for achievements
☐ ☐ Having a quiet conversation

Compare lists—then GIVE! The vast majority of couples rarely have more than one "stroke" in common—all the more reason to consider them highly, and often.

▼ *Help me, Father, this week in my giving—in ways that often are not the most familiar.*

COUNSEL—REFLECTION AND WISDOM
LOVINGLY SHARED

Listen to counsel . . . that you may be wise.
—PROV. 19:20

 *F*earing the future can consume you; feelings of inadequacy are commonplace. Will I know how to handle certain situations? Will I be prepared for life's inevitable challenges? In deep, abiding relationships, like marriage and family, wise counsel lovingly shared helps drive out these fears and lessen these inadequacies.

In a maturing relationship, we seek counsel from one another in dealing with the marriage, our children, my job, and so on. "Next time I notice you feeling so (frustrated, withdrawn, sad) what response from me would help most?" "You seem to be more patient than I am when the kids begin to (procrastinate, back-talk)—what suggestions for me would you have?" Inadequacies vulnerably shared and counsel lovingly given can expand and strengthen the marriage wonderfully.

 Heavenly Father, grant me the wisdom to seek the counsel of others who care.

COUNSEL FROM THE BOOK

The counsel of the LORD stands forever.
—PS. 33:11

*W*ise counsel has its roots in the forever wise One. Counsel based only on personal experience or impression will be flawed by human weakness. It's God's counsel, extracted from His Word and lived out in human experience, that will stand the test of time and be perfect in its wisdom. Couples seeking the wisdom of Scripture together find a oneness first in looking beyond their individual needs and then in trusting God for direction in their spiritual pilgrimage.

Teresa and I have followed the same devotional reading plan from time to time. We reflect privately on the passage and then during the course of the day share our insights with each other. Proverbs is a special favorite of ours. On several occasions throughout our marriage, we have read a chapter a day for a month. We have even spent an entire year reading and rereading counsel from Proverbs, discussing it during the day, and seeking wisdom for specific personal or family issues.

▼ *In Your light we see light (Ps. 36:9).*

YOU AND ME, BABE

So come, therefore, and let us consult together.
—NEH. 6:7

*T*here have been times in my marriage when I wanted to run to a friend for a quick fix on a problem. But God has always led me to seek His Word and my husband's counsel first.

Seeking counsel outside the marriage first can lead to further distance. "But what if my partner won't tell me anything?" I often hear. Well, think of it this way. When we lovingly challenge our spouses to give us their counsel and then receive and act on it, an atmosphere of trust and intimacy emerges. Women, thinking they are more spiritual, won't challenge their husbands with spiritual matters; they run to their pastor first. Instead of asking their mate to pray for them, they'll call a friend. Even where the kids are concerned, women sometimes feel they know more than their husband and don't seek his counsel. I believe God wanted me to seek my husband's counsel first. When I do, God then challenges David to be the leader it is in him to be.

▼ *Father, I know You can strengthen my partner spiritually better than I can.*

COUNSEL FROM AN UNEXPECTED
SOURCE—YOUR SPOUSE!

In the multitude of counselors there is safety.
—PROV. 11:14

*I*f the walls of my counseling office could talk, they would tell countless stories of people in pain and sorrow, much of it avoidable had they listened to the counsel of a caring spouse. Jack's financial future had been wrecked by a fraudulent business partnership. I remember his questioning plea: "Sarah tried to warn me! How could she have known?" Earlier, Jack had brushed off her concerns as ridiculous, feeling that she didn't know anything about business. While Sarah didn't have second sight, she could *see* things about the partnership Jack could not, a God-given sensitivity that told her "no" or at least "wait."

Though Trudy's two-month relationship with a neighbor friend had stopped short of sexual infidelity, it had almost destroyed her marriage to Jay. "Why couldn't I see what Jay saw?" Trudy asked. "He tried to tell me that our neighbor wanted more than a neighborly friendship, but I thought he was being silly." Jay could *see* things about the friendship that Trudy could not.

▼ *Thank You, God, for giving me a helpmate to see things I don't. Grant me the wisdom of receiving my partner's loving counsel.*

COMPETENT TO COUNSEL

Ointment and perfume delight the heart, And the sweetness of a man's friend gives delight by hearty counsel. —PROV. 27:9

*W*hen I was growing up, John Wayne was considered the archetypal American male. Self-sufficiency and independent thinking are the hallmarks of a "real man," and it's a sign of weakness if he admits he needs help, especially a woman's.

Well, let me admit it here in print for all the world to see: I am not a real (John Wayne) man! Why? Because I need counsel from others, and horror of horrors, I want and need counsel from my wife!

I thank God for the hundreds of times Holly has given me her views on an issue or problem I was facing. She sees things in ways that I don't, and her perspective has often made the difference between a good and bad decision.

We *need* each other's counsel in marriage. Listening to what our spouse thinks about a problem is often one of the wisest ways to go about solving it.

So seek your partner's counsel, and offer yours— your partner needs your wisdom, too.

▼ *God, help me listen to my spouse's wise counsel, and help me offer wise counsel in turn.*

WHAT SHOULD I DO, DOC?

*Without counsel, plans go awry, But in the
multitude of counselors they are established.*
—PROV. 15:22

*T*erry had a lot of problems, anyone could see that.
She was married to a non-Christian, stayed at home
with three young children, and had financial difficulties. She would eagerly ask my advice, and I was more
than willing to make suggestions for her spiritual
growth.

After weeks of constant turmoil, however, I became
concerned and frustrated by her lack of progress.

I took the situation to Chris, a psychologist, for his
thoughts. After listening patiently, he said something I
wasn't quite ready for. "Why are you trying to fix her?"
he asked. He explained that Terry was like someone
dying of thirst—all she wanted was immediate relief, not
deeper truths. I suddenly realized that my efforts to
help Terry were focused more on what I wanted to offer
than on what she needed. My husband's objective and
kind counsel showed me that I should meet Terry's
needs rather than force my agenda on her. With Chris's
advice, Terry and I are both doing better. Thanks, Doc!

▼ *God, help me seek out counsel from others, including my spouse, so that my efforts to serve You suc-
ceed.*

ASK FOR COUNSEL? YOU MUST BE KIDDING!

By pride comes nothing but strife, But with the well-advised is wisdom.
—PROV. 13:10

*E*xploratory questions in marriage help broaden our understanding of an issue and of one another. They also open us to receive counsel from a spouse. Here are samples for discussion:

- What is one way you would like me to grow in the next year?

- How could I pray for you in the next few months?

- What worry do you have about how our children are developing? Could I help?

- What is one of the most romantic times you can remember us having?

- What do you see as the two most important challenges we face this year?

- What strengths do you see in our relationship that you would like me to emphasize?

 Lord, open my heart to hear from this special partner You've given me.

COURT—TO LOVINGLY EMBRACE AND CARE FOR

A time to embrace . . .
—ECCL. 3:5

*L*oving embrace isn't just a polite sign of welcome. It's an affirmation of that person's worth and a declaration that you value the relationship. A gentle touch or countless other tender expressions of "I care" separate love relationships from mere acquaintances.

Couples are often counseled to *connect* with physical touch as they part in the morning and again as they reunite in the evening. Don't let kids, chores, or the nightly news steal away those few moments reaffirming your commitment to faithfulness and tender care.

▼ *Lord, help us show the gratitude we feel for each other in the warmth of our embrace.*

COURT ME REGULARLY!

I am lovesick . . . and his right hand embraces me.
—SONG 2:5–6

*I*t's liberating to remember that God, not people, planned this whole "boy-girl" thing of courting, marriage, and sex. This grateful reflection frees me to give lovingly to my spouse. When I lose sight of this truth, I begin to take, to become preoccupied with me and my needs. Stay grateful and enjoy the fullness of God's plan! If the tender expressions of love from your courting days cease with marriage, feelings of being taken for granted soon set in.

Dates keep romance alive. This isn't family time with your kids, or social time with other couples. A date is two people alone, doing something together for fun. Teresa and I enjoy Saturday brunch and a matinee movie, or an afternoon ice cream and "people watching" in an outdoor park, or a quiet dinner just talking. Take turns picking what you do, put a smile on your face, and go!

▼ *Lord, we thank You for the opportunity of strengthening Your plan by making time just for us.*

HOW ABOUT A DATE?

> *"Rise up, my love, my fair one,*
> *and come away!"*
> —SONG 2:10

$\mathcal{D}$avid and I missed out on courting. We married at the ripe old age of 16, then college, kids, work, and just trying to survive seemed to eat up our life together. As we've matured—in age and in our love—we see that we have short-changed our relationship.

This became clear after a trip we took to just play and relax. David was so attentive and really went out of his way to make our trip enjoyable. I loosened up and allowed him to take the lead. All this courting felt really good, but when we got home, we were soon back to our old ways: David preoccupied with everything but me; me trying to control everything. That short trip showed us that courting is not just a once-a-week date after you're married. Courting is taking the time every day to say I love you in a lot of small ways. Remember way back before you married how you acted and felt toward each other? Courting can rekindle that spark and make us feel special again.

▼ *Father, You sought us first to spend time with us; help me to have the same initiative with my spouse.*

FUN FOR ALL AGES

Then her husband arose and went after her,
to speak kindly to her. —JUDG. 19:3

Sheila and Walt had been married 50 years when they flew in to participate in one of our "marriage intensive" sessions. Together, they had enjoyed raising their children, growing in their faith, building a business, and traveling the globe, but their marriage lacked romance and affectionate courting. Something held Sheila back, while Walt's feelings of rejection compounded his workaholic tendencies and resulted in occasional outbreaks of intense anger. Sheila's hurt and loneliness increased, and thus the cycle continued.

Two days into our work the couple began to find freedom and healing from decades of pent-up hurt. The next day Sheila revealed a traumatic and abusive childhood experience that she had not shared with anyone for over 60 years. Walt wept with his new understanding of Sheila's indifference to affection. By the time of the couple's scheduled Saturday night "date" affection was enjoyable to both. "Courting" had returned!

Truly understanding your spouse—which takes time to listen and empathy to comfort—is a vital part of a romantic, courting relationship.

▼ *Lord, might Your plan for our "oneness" be all that*
You desire it to be—spirit, soul, and body.

AH, THE WONDER OF BEING IN LOVE

Husbands, love your wives, just as Christ also loved the church.
—EPH. 5:25

I remember the first time I saw Holly. We were students at the University of Texas. *"Wow!"* I thought. For a long time, I was too shy to ask her out, though my insecurities didn't keep me from going by where she worked on campus as often as I could. It was always exciting to find her there and talk with her before my next class called me away.

Finally, I mustered enough courage to ask her out. We had a great time. She was fun, a great listener, and a very genuine person. Our relationship continued to grow over the months that we dated, and soon we were hooked on each other.

During our courtship, one of those special little things we did for each other was to leave messages on each other's car windshield. Each day at the end of classes I would head toward the parking lot hoping Holly had left me a note. It was a small gesture that meant the world to me, and I would return the favor as often as I could.

Messages left on a car windshield to show how much I care. . . . Twelve years of marriage later, I don't do that very often. I think I'll leave a message on her windshield today!

▼ *God, help me to continue to court my spouse even though we have already walked down the aisle.*

FLOWERS? FOR ME?

*"Rise up, my love, my fair one,
and come away!"*
—SONG 2:10

*R*emember how you treated your spouse when you were dating? Remember those actions, small and large, that told you how special you were to each other? You can still court, even though you're married.

Ever since I can remember, Chris has brought me flowers whenever he returns home from a trip, along with a carefully selected gift for each child. For our part, the kids and I tape a big "Welcome Home" sign decorated with streamers and balloons to the door so it is the first thing he sees as he pulls into the garage.

We've done this countless times and still get a kick out of it. The kids are learning a valuable lesson, too. They see how a husband and wife need to treat each other, how to act like sweethearts. This treasured tradition of ours is one that says, as our daughter Ashley puts it, "Daddy, we'd marry you all over again."

How long has it been since you sent a card to your spouse or called to say "I love you"? Do it today—the response will be worth it.

 God, help us to continually court each other, in ways that show just how special our marriage is.

COURTING CAN LEAD TO LOVE MAPS!

How beautiful and how delightful you are,
My love, with all your charms!
—SONG 7:6 NASB

*H*elen and Jeff did these Love Map exercises to deepen their courting of each other into a special passionate closeness.

First they considered what a perfect, sexually intimate time with each other would include. Then they listed at least ten preferences, including timing, location, and clothing. After they completed their Love Maps, they chose a private time and place to exchange them. They discussed them as much as they were comfortable doing and answered each other's questions. Finally, they scheduled two times of intimacy to fulfill both Love Maps (planning created anticipation.) Jeff first fulfilled Helen's Love Map. Then, they planned a time for Helen to fulfill Jeff's.

The Love Map exercise will help you as you court each other. Throughout the day, spend moments anticipating the pleasures of the two of you "becoming one." Freely share all of yourselves with each other.

▼ *Teach to me to give all of myself to my spouse—spirit, soul, and body.*

DEFERENCE—TO YIELD TO OTHERS
FOR THEIR BENEFIT

*. . . submitting to one another in the fear
of God.*
—EPH. 5:21

*E*ach of us seems to have our own agenda in life that can easily absorb all our attention. When this happens, we lose sight of others and their needs. I might become so controlling that I cram my agenda down your throat! To defer is to yield to you, to become aware, caring, and supportive.

Submission or deferring is never a one-way street. God doesn't appoint some to submit and some to "lord it over" others! A yielded heart is a mark of the Spirit's work, uniquely divine and impossible to sustain by flesh alone. After too many years, I finally began to see the wisdom of heeding Teresa's impressions about our children's needs and her hunches to avoid certain business deals. We can trust the Lord to bring the peace of "oneness" to two hearts that forge a common bond of deference, protecting each from much pain and providing great security.

▼ *Father, I see the wisdom of yielding to You and therefore to my partner, for the benefit of those I love.*

GIVING YOURSELF UP

Jesus Christ . . . did not consider it robbery to be equal with God, but made Himself of no reputation . . . and coming in the likeness of men.
—PHIL. 2:5–7

$\mathcal{I}$'m sure glad Christ didn't selfishly hold on to heaven! I'm glad He deferred to my world and my needs, thinking them more important than His own. Such deference is what God's giving must look like, and such giving is what God's love must look like. Deference always implies giving up "my" way or "my" plans. In light of eternity, how important could my agenda be anyway? How much more important to love you by letting it go.

I still remember the impact Ephesians 5:25 had on me some twenty years back: "Husbands love your wives as Christ also loved the church and *gave Himself* for her." What had I *given* for Teresa? Not, Had I worked a lot and tried to provide an adequate living, but, What had I sacrificed? The silence was deafening, convicting: Nothing! From that moment, God began to gently reveal that my selfishness was harming my wife, that I was sloppy, and procrastinated. The giving up of myself was underway!

▼ *Lord, use my marriage to perfect in me Christlikeness; don't hold back your hand from reshaping my life according to your pleasure.*

LET'S MOVE

Even a fool is counted wise when he holds his peace; when he shuts his lips, he is considered perceptive. —PROV. 17:28

$\mathscr{D}$avid and I went away for spring break to one of our favorite hotels. When we got to our room, we discovered it was not the one David had requested. But our next room had no view! Finally, the next day, the third room that David had asked for, the one with the view, was ready for us.

I could have made a big deal of moving three times in a day and a half, but it was important to David. I chose to defer to his wishes. The move took all of 15 minutes; even more important was the reassurance David had of my support.

▼ *Lord, help me to know those times when my spouse truly needs my silent understanding and support more than my opinion.*

DEFERENCE TO ANOTHER'S "AGENDA"

"I am the vine, you are the branches."
—JOHN 15:5

*F*or years, I didn't understand that Teresa's childhood in a large family with six children—three of them deaf—was often lonely. Who would give priority to her interests? Who would defer to her needs? "No one" was usually the answer. No wonder she grew up feeling left out. I didn't realize when we married that she needed me to play this "deferring" role, to look out for her best interests. I thought my role was to make a living for us!

Teresa wasn't actually aware of what she needed either. Over time and by much trial and error, we both came to see that inner joy and marital closeness didn't come through possessions or accomplishments. Simpler things sufficed: deferring to another's agenda—for a lifetime or just a day. Taking the initiative! Ask, "Since we have this Saturday free, how would *you* like to spend it? I'd like it to be fun for you."

▼ *Father, thinking more often about others than I do about myself doesn't come naturally; help me.*

I'LL GET UP. NO, I'LL GET UP. NO, I'LL GET UP.

Let no one seek his own, but each one the other's well-being. —1 COR. 10:24

*H*ave you ever played the "Who is going to get up and take care of the baby at three in the morning?" game? Let me describe it for you.

You and your spouse are dead tired from the daily rigors of life, liberty, and the pursuit of happiness. The baby went to sleep a few hours ago and you have both nodded off, when that little bundle of joy decides it is time to interact again. You lie there pretending you are sound asleep, hoping and praying your spouse will get up and feed and diaper the baby.

Holly and I have played that game hundreds of times—I don't know of a married couple with kids that hasn't. Yet more often than not, Holly is the one who shakes off sleep to meet our baby's needs.

That doesn't sound like much of a sacrifice, but it is huge in its implications. It is her way of putting sacrificial love into practice. That is love, and it isn't easy, especially when you are tired, or feel unloved, or have already gone the distance for someone who hasn't returned the favor. Yet that is what God wants us to be willing to do. That kind of love changes you, makes you more willing to give. It leads by example, and it asks nothing in return.

▼ *God, help me defer to my partner's needs, even at three in the morning.*

YOUR WAY OR MINE?

But the wisdom that is from above is . . . willing to yield. —JAMES 3:17

I'll never forget the New Year's Eve when we had nothing planned except dinner out. I had set my heart on going to see "The Nutcracker Suite." But when I had mentioned this to Chris, he said something like "I'd rather die!"

After dinner that night, Chris presented me with two tickets for the "Nutcracker." He had thought it over and decided that if it was something I really wanted to do, then he wanted to make it happen. I was thrilled. Not only did he surprise me with the two tickets, he also went with a gracious attitude, as if he really wanted to go.

If you have ever gone somewhere with an unwilling spouse, you know how important attitude is. Everyone and his dog will soon know how unhappy he or she is, making the time together miserable. Chris hadn't changed his mind about the ballet, but he showed how much he cared about me by putting my desires over his.

Marriage can become a battleground if we don't defer appropriately and lovingly to our spouse's needs and desires. This may be hard to do at times, especially with a good attitude. But it clearly shows how much your partner matters, and in the process, we learn to be a truly loving spouse.

▼ *God, help me to yield to my spouse's wishes whenever possible, and in doing so, learn to mature in my ability to love.*

DEFERRING THROUGH SHARING YOUR "WISHES"

In honor [give] preference to one another.
—ROM. 12:10

$\mathcal{A}$s we counseled with Sheri and Bob, they learned a few tips to help them "defer" to another's wishes. First, they prepared "wish" lists that included specific, positive ideas such as, "I'm hoping you might become more comfortable initiating affection," and "I wish we would not criticize each other in front of others—particularly our children."

Then they shared their lists with each other. This helped them avoid the destructive cycle of having expectations of each other, and not communicating their wishes and then becoming hurt or angry when their expectations weren't met! Clarifying "wishes" guards us from the pain of dealing in negative generalities. It also helps us bridle the tongue until we've formulated a positive wish.

Take time to list six wishes. Exchange lists if it will help you remember some of your partner's desires. Then defer to your partner in seeking to fulfill wishes as God directs and empowers you.

▼ *Thanks, Father, for the strength to look beyond myself and give to this special one You've blessed me with.*

DEVOTION—A FIRM AND DEPENDABLE FOUNDATION OF COMMITTED CARE

Be kindly affectionate to one another with brotherly love.
                                        —ROM. 12:10

*D*evotion makes care predictable. The loving care and concern that can be counted upon gives a relationship a secure foundation. Truly, the devotion of perfect love casts out all fear.

Too many relationships ride the roller-coaster of "caring" then "not caring." The caring high feels good, but the low of not caring is devastating. Devoted love protects us from the pit of not caring. We often see couples who have enjoyed some great times together, but once one or the other feels rejected, let down, betrayed, or abandoned in some way, the bottom falls out of the relationship—and the good memories and positive things fall out too. Often this is because present marital hurt taps a reservoir of unresolved hurt from the past— from childhood, parents, or former marriages. Counseling addresses this reservoir of unhealed pain. It's scary to look at old painful issues, however, and progress depends on daily caring devotion within the marriage.

▼ *Lord, sensitize me to daily opportunities to care.*

DEVOTION FROM THE CROSS

*For the joy that was set before Him endured
the cross.*
—HEB. 12:2

$\mathscr{D}$evotion kept Christ on the cross, devotion to His
Father and to His Father's love for me. His devoted
commitment was not unexpected, however. He had
been faithful in small, everyday things, and so was prepared for this climax of human history.

Couples often come to counseling in the aftermath of
life's tragedies: a baby lost in labor, bankruptcy, a rebellious teenager. None of us is exempt from life's pain, but
two distinct patterns emerge as couples face it: Tragedy
draws some couples together, while tearing others
apart. The difference between couples who survive
tragedy, actually experiencing deeper closeness, and
those who don't seems to be daily devotion to the "little" things. Couples who survive are the ones who depart lovingly in the morning; express their love in words,
notes, and small acts of kindness; talk, listen, spend
time together. These "little" things offer the assurance
that if something major comes along, "you can count on
me."

▼ *Father, help me to remember that there are no little
things in love.*

FIRST THINGS FIRST

To everything there is a season, A time for every purpose under heaven.

—ECCL. 3:1

*B*arbara, my pastor's wife, is blessed with a women's retreat ministry that reaches thousands each year. Her success could easily prevent her from supporting Harold and their ministry in our church. Yet her devotion to Harold is the reason God can trust her with His work in this ministry.

Fifteen years ago, before I started doing women's retreats, I was asked what goals I had as a housewife. At the time, I hadn't even thought of having goals. My life goals have slowly broadened to devotion to God, husband, children, and, finally, others.

So often I hear women complain, "I don't have a ministry" or "I don't have anything to give." God has given us a special ministry—our husbands and then our children. When our duties to them are carried out to God's satisfaction, He will free us for ministry to the outside world.

▼ *Lord, guide me in the right ways of devotion.*

BE DEVOTED TO ME AS YOUR FRIEND

"No longer do I call you servants . . . but I have called you friends." —JOHN 15:15

*I*n the early years of our marriage, we set priorities according to the "squeaking-wheel" plan. "As soon as I take care of this," we'd say, "we'll be together," but the urgent demands from work, friends, church, and the kids never stopped. Our time never came.

Ten years into our marriage, the barrenness of a busy life began to take its toll. We gave ourselves the advice we gave other couples: "Schedule a weekly time to talk, don't leave it to chance." If the time had to change each week, we'd spend Sunday evening discussing schedules. We listened to one another's ideas and wishes. We worked together in our parenting. We developed goals for our marriage and family. Gradually, we began to sense more teamwork, more friendship.

Friends make time for one another. You can't be close to someone who is not there!

▼ *Lord, even as You became a true friend to me and devoted time to me, may I be a friend to my spouse also.*

WHEN I'M SIXTY-FOUR

*And let our people also learn to maintain
good works.*   —TITUS 3:14

$\mathscr{I}$ grew up listening to the Beatles, and the song I find myself humming every so often is "When I'm Sixty-Four." One of the lines asks, "Will you still need me, . . . when I'm sixty-four?"

That is something most married couples wonder about, isn't it? Will my spouse still want to be with me when my wrinkles are set in concrete, my hair is gray (if I have any left), and my step a little slower? Will my spouse still love me and want to be around? Scary question, isn't it?

In a day and age when few things seem permanent, and people change partners like they change shirts, we all wonder if love will last. Yet true intimacy is built on the commitment to love your partner forever.

When I'm sixty-four, I plan to be married to the same person, and Holly feels the same way. Regardless of how bumpy life gets, that's the way we want it be—and the way God wants it to be. We aren't just marking time, either. We want the long haul to be as fruitful and joyous as it possibly can. So does God. That is why He does everything He can to help us.

Sixty-four, no matter what. How about you?

▼ *God, help us remain devoted to each other no matter how rough things get in our marriage.*

I'LL BE THERE

*Now set your heart and your soul to seek the
LORD your God.* —1 CHRON. 22:19

$\mathcal{A}$s an elderly couple sat in the cafeteria last night laughing and smiling throughout their conversation, I marveled at how much they were enjoying each other. Chris smiled and told the kids, "There go your Mom and Dad thirty years from now." They said, "Oh, gross!" and made fun, but we know the point got across.

When my Grandmom became disabled, my Grandad cared for her for six years. Until her death, he loved to take her everywhere and do all he could for her.

Devotion, to me, means emotional investment and interest in your spouse over time, no matter what. It is a sign of maturity and goes much deeper than mere actions. You can't just *act* devoted. The hardships of life will crush that out of you. You have to *be* devoted—you have to make it part of your character. Real devotion is dependable, foundational, and of God.

Devotion isn't just the province of older couples, but there is something to be said for the test of time.

Are you really devoted to your spouse? Are you in the marriage "for better or for worse"? Can your spouse count on you for a lifetime?

▼ *God, please help me develop a lifetime devotion to my spouse that is grounded in Your love.*

DEVOTED TO REMOVING MARRIAGE LIES

Bringing every thought into captivity to the obedience of Christ. —2 COR. 10:5

*W*hy should I change?" insisted Ellen. "I thought marriage meant I was okay just like I am." Ellen and Dale suffered from several marriage misconceptions or "lies." For many reasons, most couples begin their lives together believing several lies. These are not lies that these couples would consciously admit to believing, which makes confronting the lies more difficult. With Ellen and Dale we discussed the lie that "I shouldn't have to change." We discussed the truth that we must be accepting while at the same time our personal maturity and growth require changes in us—it's what the process of "Christ-likeness" is all about.

We often suggest that during one of their established weekly times to talk, couples discuss various "lies" they find themselves thinking. Typical marriage lies include: It's all your fault; If it takes hard work, we must not be right for each other; You owe me; and You should be like me.

Identifying lies in your thinking is helpful in building closeness. Set aside time this week to take turns sharing the lies you are most vulnerable to and reassure each other with the truth in each case: It's not all your fault— I have much to work on. The truth is we're very right for each other.

▼ *Help me, Father, to take lies captive and cast them down, replacing them with truth.*

DISCIPLINE—TO REPROVE AND CORRECT WHEN LIMITS ARE EXCEEDED

Do not withhold correction . . .
—PROV. 13:13

I need discipline? What a strange thought, until you realize that discipline means setting boundaries so that you won't get hurt. God sets limits, and crossing them may result in blessings missed by being "off-course," or loss of intimacy with my Master.

The "tough" side of love is sometimes hard to accept. Teresa understands it better than I. For years I tended to spoil the children, but the softer I got with the kids, the tougher she'd get. Then I'd get softer! We were driving ourselves apart over discipline. Gradually I began to see the benefits of saying no, of giving warnings and issuing consequences. Boundaries gave security, which reduced tension. The children were freer to enjoy life inside those boundaries, rather than spend all their energy testing them!

▼ *Thanks, Father, for showing me the good side of tough love.*

THE DISCIPLINE OF LOVE

As many as I love, I rebuke and chasten.
—REV. 3:19

*G*od's discipline reminds me that I'm part of His family. It is loving correction for right-living, though—not punishment for wrong-doing. Discipline looks to the future, while punishment focuses on the past. Early in my Christian journey, I thought God's discipline seemed harsh at times; in maturity, I've been chastened merely by knowing that my heavenly Father is grieved.

In the past few years, the wounded look on Teresa's face has been sufficient to let me know I've failed her in some way: perhaps an impatient response to a loving inquiry, or a broken promise. It now hurts me deeply to know that I've hurt her. As God saddens my heart, contriteness gives way to confession—to Him and to her. Fellowship and intimacy are restored. Thus gratitude for the security of this love, rather than fear, motivates me to change.

▼ *Thank You, God, for a love that cares enough to discipline.*

YOU'RE TOO EASY

Blows that hurt cleanse away evil, As do stripes the inner depths of the heart.
—PROV. 20:30

*F*inding a compromise between love and limits can be a real test for parents. So many obstacles must be overcome in trying to discipline our children. David and I have found our parenting skills are often born out of how we were raised. My parents spanked; David's talked or grounded. So we approached discipline in our home in opposite ways. Our kids needed the security of our being one in our dealing with discipline.

We did a lot wrong in the beginning, and we had to learn how to deal with each child differently. David and I also learned that unresolved conflict between us would affect how we dealt with the kids. As we have learned to heal our marriage hurts, we no longer use disciplining the kids as a battleground. As we've grown together as a couple, we have learned to balance each other in discipline.

▼ *Father, help us to prioritize so that we can give to our family out of love, not anger.*

THE DISCIPLINE OF NATURAL CONSEQUENCES

*Even if some do not okay the word, they,
without a word, may be won.*
—1 PET. 3:1

I wonder if it might be good to slow down a little on these corners?" But since Teresa didn't insist, I ignored her. I was in a hurry for an important conference and speeding seemed justified. It was time for the discipline of natural consequences; share a concern in a loving way then back off and let nature take over! Around the next turn a speed trap was waiting for a husband ignoring his wife's counsel. The ticket was written, and silence filled several miles. Not even an "I told you so." I was miserable. The discipline of natural consequences had worked its work in a sorrow deeply felt, apologies made, and fines paid. My repentance is not total, but progress is being made.

The ministry of caring counsel and a quiet spirit can be greatly used by the Lord. In an accepting silence, the Spirit's conviction is almost deafening.

▼ *Lord, might the quietness of my spouse's acceptance ... in spite of failure ... empower my listening to Your voice.*

PRESS ON TO THE MARK

*Poverty and shame will come to him who
    disdains correction;
But he who regards a rebuke will be honored.*
—PROV. 13:18

$\mathcal{T}$hink of some of the greatest inventions—the light bulb, the telephone, and the airplane to name a few. They all have at least one thing in common—it took hundreds of "failed" efforts before final success was achieved. In a very real sense, when inventors try something that doesn't work, they haven't really failed. They have successfully found out what doesn't work and can move on to try something else.

We husbands and wives are inventors. We are inventing one of the most important products of all—intimacy. We may try and fail numerous times for every success, but each failure can be used to find a better path.

The task of creating intimacy in marriage is quite a challenge, and discipline is essential. We need to keep trying to achieve that goal no matter how often we fail. Like any committed inventor, we keep trying until the light bulb illuminates, the telephone rings, and the airplane flies. We are to let nothing get in our way.

▼ *God, help me be disciplined, "pressing on to the mark" in my efforts to be intimate.*

STOP, LOOK, LISTEN

He who keeps instruction is in the way of life
—PROV. 10:17

*C*hris and I have totally different driving styles. I'm pretty laid back—if someone rides my bumper, I move over. If a driver honks his horn, it won't ruin my day. Chris takes the actions of other drivers a bit more personally. If someone rides his bumper, he becomes angry, as if the driver has just kidnapped his children. If he had the James Bond car for one day, he would take it out on the highway and oil slick people into oblivion.

I've told him I'm concerned about the way he drives. I'm not ready to go to heaven just yet. The other reason is that our kids are watching. Chris listened, but his driving didn't change.

Then, one day, our son, Matthew, was driving with us in the car and said to Chris, "Dad, hurry up—don't let that guy get in front of you!" God used that comment to convict Chris to be more disciplined in handling his emotions and actions on the road.

God uses a variety of ways to point out the changes we need to make. Our son's simple comment became a strong reminder to Chris that his lack of discipline while driving was being noticed, and it was enough to help him grow more serious about driving. That is the loving discipline our heavenly Father shows to us about the many ways we are not disciplined. We all need it.

▼ *God, help me learn to be disciplined in expressing my feelings toward my spouse.*

DISCIPLINE FROM COMMON SPIRITUAL GOALS

The word of God is living and powerful, and sharper than any two-edged sword.

—HEB. 4:12

*T*eresa and I have found that deepening our spiritual closeness was very difficult but extremely rewarding. For years our spiritual intimacy consisted of sitting on the same church pew. Gradually we began to develop common spiritual goals. As we began getting closer to God, we felt closer to each other. Goals for spiritual growth we've shared include reading through the entire New Testament during the year (one chapter a day will more than do it); memorizing ten Scripture passages on communication (Eph. 4:29; Prov. 10:19; 12:18; 12:25; 15:1–28; 16:23; 17:27; 19:13; 25:24); and working together on topical Bible studies. (*The Healthy Christian Life* by Minirth, Meier, Meier, and Hawkins is a good one.)

▼ *Father, draw us together in a fresh vision for spiritual oneness.*

EDIFICATION—PROMOTING GROWTH AND DEVELOPMENT

Let us pursue the things which make for peace and the things by which one may edify another.
—ROM. 14:19

I'm excited to be with you as you give me loving care. Criticize me and I may begin to avoid you. I feel built up when you seem glad to see me or compliment a strength you see in me. If you comment positively on progress you've seen me make, I feel good and even more motivated.

Often I begin my counseling sessions asking for the following report: "Share with me something positive you've noticed in your marriage relationship since we were last together." My purpose is twofold. First, I hope to encourage the couple to develop a positive mind-set, to anticipate and look for positive interactions. Second, I want each partner to experience the encouragement in a spouse's good report . . . sometimes even "bragging" about a spouse's behavior or change. These results tend to produce a more positive, encouraging home.

▼ *Lord, remove my "half-empty" view of life.*

THE EDIFYING POWER OF WORDS

Let no corrupt word proceed out of your mouth, but what is good for necessary edification.
—EPH. 4:29

*T*aking this verse seriously might make a difference in the words that come out of my mouth. I try to filter them through this "filter": if this comment will build someone up, I say it; if not, I don't. Research confirms that it takes ten to twelve positive "strokes" to build me up to a receptivity to even one message of constructive criticism! Too many homes have ten to twelve critical messages for every positive one! Might the "atmosphere" of our home be one of edification.

Heaven will likely reveal the power of our words. The challenge of edifying words is one of "speaking the truth in love" (Eph. 4:15). Two extremes are common: (1) share the truth, but not in love, and (2) hide the truth. A common marital cycle is to "hide" the truth until I can't stand it any longer and explode! "You're a slob!" or "I'd really appreciate help picking up the bedroom; I really need you." Which would you rather hear?

▼ *Lord, station a guard at my lips to speak only things that edify.*

STINKIN' THINKIN'

The wise woman builds her house, But the foolish pulls it down with her hands.
—PROV. 14:1

*W*omen can tear down with their hands but also with their words. We've all heard the joke "if Momma ain't happy, ain't nobody happy." I've seen this to be true in our home. When I am critical or tear down with my words, I can see this attitude passed on to the kids. I can listen to their conversations and they can sound just like my own negative and critical attitude. To edify the ones in my home, I must change my "stinkin' thinkin'." Such negative and critical thinking is usually the result of my unhealed hurts. When I've let hurts fester, the thoughts I have are going to be negative and critical. To be able to edify, I need to heal these hurts and release my anger through forgiving the ones who have hurt me. Being free to build up those I care most about is exciting!

▼ *Father, help me to release my hurts and forgive so I can be a positive person.*

EDIFICATION IS SOMETIMES SILENT

[Be] slow to speak.
—JAMES 1:19

"Don't forget to pick up the bathroom before you leave." The more Teresa reminded me to pick up after myself, the less I did it. We'd had this conflict for almost twelve years, and we'd made no progress toward resolution.

Then one Monday morning, a miracle occurred. The reminding stopped. I left my side of the bathroom in a total mess and went to work, almost proud I had outlasted Teresa. I returned that evening to my messy countertop and to a second miracle. Teresa was in a good mood and affectionate, and she never mentioned the mess.

She told me later she realized she had focused on my behavior instead of just accepting me. She prayed about her attitude, and God led her to ask, "Will this issue matter ten years from now? Will it matter in eternity?" She also realized God could be trusted to bring changes He thought necessary.

A few days later, a third miracle took place. I began to want to put away my mess. Teresa's loving silence had helped me hear God's prompting, which brought edification. The war was over, and our marriage had won.

▼ *Heavenly Father, if this thing that irritates me is important to You, I'll trust You to bring the changes. I know You can do a much better job than I can.*

I WANT TO BUILD YOU UP

The tongue of the righteous is choice silver.
—PROV. 10:20

Since moving to Austin recently, we have watched our home being built from the ground up. The contractors cleared the lot, laid the foundation, framed, sheetrocked, painted, and carpeted. We enjoyed going to see it every few days and see progress.

Our builder is a good one, and everything he did added to the house and moved it toward completion. He didn't clear the lot one day and then trash it out the next. He didn't lay the foundation one day and then jackhammer it to smithereens the next.

The building process has been a great picture of how I am supposed to treat Holly. Everything I do is supposed to build her up. Each word spoken or action taken is supposed to add to her life, not tear it down.

Build up, not tear down. That is part of our job description as a joint "builder" in marriage. And, remember, God has to be the ultimate construction manager; otherwise we labor in vain.

In your marriage are you doing more building up or tearing down? Are you allowing God to be the construction manager?

▼ *God, please help me to build my spouse up. Help me rely on You so that I don't labor in vain.*

BUILD UP, NOT DOWN

*Let each of us please his neighbor for his
good, leading to edification.*
—ROM. 15:2

*H*ave you ever been around a couple who spent most
of their time putting each other down? Not overtly, mind
you, but in subtle ways. Things like making a joke at the
person's expense, bringing up an embarrassing story
about them, speaking to them in a condescending tone
of voice, and shooting down their opinions as if they
were imbicilic. It can be pretty uncomfortable. When
you are that couple, it can be even more uncomfortable.

Edification is a fancy word that means to build up, to
promote the growth and development of another. Have
you ever been around a couple that edified each other?
They are a little hard to find. Instead of tension, there is
harmony. Instead of pain, there is healing. Instead of
fear, there is comfort. This kind of couple is a joy.

God wants our marriages to be a place where edification is central. We are to build one another up, not tear
down. We are to look for ways to help the person grow
into maturity, not get in the way. Easy to talk about, hard
to do.

Are you a builder?

▼ *God, help me look for ways to build my spouse up
each day. I want to be a builder.*

EDIFY THROUGH SHARING
THE TRUTH IN LOVE

Let no corrupt communication proceed out of your mouth.
—EPH. 4:29

*T*eresa and I have worked diligently over the last several years on simply how we talk to each other—desiring to speak only wholesome words.

First, before I speak I check to make sure that the purpose of my words is to edify—*"only such a word as is edifying."* To edify is to build up, to encourage and esteem another person. It's not time for me to talk if my purpose is to hurt, attack, or defend my position. Second, before I speak I discern the need for my words—*"according to the need. . . ."* There should be a need for my words before they're spoken! This is why listening to Teresa is so important, trying to see things from her perspective. Third, I try to make sure the timing of my words is right—*"of the moment."* Teresa's receptivity is often directly related to the timing of my sharing. We've found that quality times of weekly talk are so important, because we can give each other undivided attention.

Begin a review this week of wholesome words, desiring to speak only words that minister grace to those who hear.

▼ *Heavenly Father, filter my words so that only wholesome words come forth.*

ENCOURAGEMENT—TO URGE FORWARD AND POSITIVELY PERSUADE TOWARD A GOAL

Therefore encourage one another.
—1 THESS. 5:11, NASB

*E*ncouragement is one of the true blessings of relationship. Without it, my life may be just as focused and my efforts just as commendable . . . but I enjoy them alone! Growing weary in doing good is sometimes a human frailty, but growing weary alone is tragic. In my weariness, I need encouragement. A beautiful closeness develops as a couple comes to count upon each other's encouragement regardless of the obstacles.

Couples coming for counsel often have an interesting view of encouragement. Many would basically say you give encouragement only when you see your spouse about to give up in some endeavor or relationship. In other words, encouragement is a fire extinguisher to be used as a last resort. Nothing is further from the true meaning of the word. Encouragement is continued gratitude for your spouse. As you feel your gratitude, you encourage!

▼ *Father, produce in our home an atmosphere of gratitude that springs forth into encouragement.*

ENCOURAGING GOOD DEEDS

Let us consider one another in order to stir up love and good works. —HEB. 10:24

*W*hat a joy it is to play a role in a spouse's flourishing in positive growth . . . pushed on by my encouragement. The seeds of encouragement spring forth into the fruits of love and good deeds. Encouragement might come verbally or in a special note. It might come on the heels of a personal victory or in a valley of discouragement. It might come privately during a quiet talk or publicly.

Couples who come to counseling wanting increased intimacy or "oneness" are often surprised at how encouragement fits in. Many lack a deep sense of intimacy because of two relatively independent, self-reliant existences. They may each have careers, or one is career-focused and the other more home-focused. Discovering the power of encouragement can help bring them together. Thus, "my career" becomes our career. You share my efforts at home through your encouragement.

▼ *Might we enjoy the closeness that mutual encouragement brings.*

ALL FOR ONE, ONE FOR ALL

Say to those who are fearful hearted,
"Be strong, do not fear."
—ISA. 35:3–4

*E*ric, our only son, was to graduate in May 1992. He needed to get some extra credits to graduate. Eric's least favorite subject, English, was one of those missing credits. He had to take it by correspondence. To say he needed our encouragement was an understatement. Completing his English project took David, me, his sister Terri, and his grandmother.

We all watched for the mail to see if we had received a grade on the last paper he'd mailed in.

When it was time to take his test, we all encouraged him to do his best. After what seemed like an eternity, we received his test results. He'd passed!

Our family will always have fond memories of working toward the common goal of Eric's graduation. No one felt, "It's your problem, you solve it."

We all feel the peace of knowing that when one Ferguson needs help, we're all ready to pitch in.

▼ *Lord, thank You for giving me such a special family.*

ENCOURAGING SEXUAL INTIMACY

Behold you are fair, my love!
Behold you are fair!
—SONG 4:1

*J*anice and her husband, Steve, often found themselves in conflict over sex, comparing their frequency with the "average." They had tried to bargain their way to a solution, trading one more sexual encounter for a dinner date or cleaning out the garage. It had not worked and Steve was often angry over Janice's lack of sexual desire.

How tragic to take the God-designed plan for "two becoming one flesh" and reduce it to numbers. Questions like "how long has it been?" or "how often should we have sex?" are common among couples we see.

In an individual session with Janice, Steve's emotional need for being found sexually "desirable" was discussed. Janice agreed to try an experiment that week. As Jim left for work, Janice sent him off with tenderness and touch, saying to him, "I'd sure like to be together with you tonight. Can we plan on it?" Steve later reported he was shocked but excited.

Janice's initiative really encouraged Steve. It began to answer his inner longing to know his wife found him sexually desirable. His "pressuring" of Janice subsided, and the frequency struggles diminished.

▼ *Father, with Your perfect love, empower me to take the initiative to love.*

IT WILL BE FINE

> *But exhort one another daily, while it is*
> *called "Today," lest any of you be hardened*
> *through the deceitfulness of sin.*
> —HEB. 3:13

Holly and I are building a home. Man, there are a million decisions to make, and none of them seem very easy. And, if you are perfectionistic like Holly and I are, each decision has to be the absolute best one.

On more than a few occasions, something wasn't done quite to my liking, and I found myself getting upset. You know, kind of a "This is the end of the world" reaction to something like a light fixture not being hung perfectly.

Dozens of times, Holly has said, "It will be fine" when I was in one of those overreactive moods. Those words were what the doctor ordered, and I often found myself handling my feelings better because of her encouragement.

I appreciate Holly's calming influence when I am feeling troubled or upset. It means a lot to have her perspective and soothing words brought into the emotional storms I sometimes create. Those storms often calm down because of what she does to help, and I am able to see things more clearly. Encouragement—what a critically important need in marriage. Offer some to your spouse today.

▼ *God, help me be encouraging to my spouse, especially when times are the toughest.*

IT'S NEVER TOO LATE

Therefore comfort each other and edify one another.
                                        —1 THESS. 5:11

$\mathcal{A}$s a child, I had a best friend named Lana. We did everything together.

A new girl moved into our neighborhood and began a friendship with Lana. I felt really hurt and reacted by deciding to have nothing to do with them. I only wanted Lana for my friend, and I didn't want her to have any other friends.

So, one day I told Lana that I couldn't be her friend anymore. I'll never forget the hurt in her eyes as she walked away. But I didn't budge.

Chris knows my shame and hurt for my childish cruelty. He reminds me how painful regret can be to carry around, and he often suggests that I track her down and tell her how bad I feel for what I did. He encourages me to face something painful in my life because he wants the best for me.

I saw Lana the other day. I think I will give her a call.

▼ *God, help me to encourage my spouse and accept encouragement.*

ENCOURAGEMENT FROM MARRIAGE AND FAMILY GOAL SETTING

Where there is no vision, the people are unrestrained. —PROV. 29:18 NASB

*T*eresa and I began to observe a degree of aimlessness after ten or so years of marriage; routine and boredom had set in; we were very busy with activity but much of it had little real joy. We came to find that King Solomon, the writer of Proverbs, was indeed wise. What was needed was a *vision*—a fresh sense of direction and destiny, a guiding framework around which we could make decisions and set objectives.

We began to use exploratory questions to help identify specific goals we wanted to accomplish. Then we focused on working together and encouraging each other to accomplish them.

During our sharing times we used questions like: In what two key ways would you like to see me grow personally in the next year? What is a concern you have about each of our children? What is an important item you'd like to see emphasized in our romance? What improvements or changes would you most like to see around our home? As we explored together some of our wishes and dreams, many of them became common goals; mutual encouragement and the joy of a fresh vision felt great.

▼ *Encourage me, Father, with a vision for my marriage—and then make me an encourager as we seek the vision together.*

ENJOYMENT—FULFILLMENT IN ANOTHER'S COMPANY

Trust . . . in the living God who gives us richly all things to enjoy. —1 TIM. 6:17

*G*od is "pro" enjoyment! Remember His conversation with Adam in Genesis 2? It was not good to be alone. Adam needed a helpmate; a companion to enjoy God's creation with. It's important to remember that God thought up this "helpmate" plan; it wasn't man's idea or society's invention. God wanted Adam to experience the deep joy of a relationship. Enjoying another person comes to focus not so much upon what we're doing . . . but simply on being together.

Teresa and I have developed numerous common interests over many years of marriage. Early the enjoyment seemed to come from the shared activity. We went through a time when we thought the activities needed to become more and more entertaining and exciting so we didn't get bored! Age, maturity, or maybe deepened companionship has brought us to a joy coming more from just being together, enjoying one another's company, sharing the experience of togetherness.

▼ *Thanks, Father, for the joy of companionship.*

GOD DID GOOD!

"He did good . . . filling our hearts with food and gladness." —ACTS 14:17

$\mathcal{G}$od did good! He did good because that's His nature. He's not a celestial kill-joy but a caring Father who desires every good thing for us. He longs for us to come to enjoy everything pertaining to life and godliness. Enjoying another person is a special part of God's plan for marriage. God "did good" when He created your partner—just for you!

Many couples come to counseling thinking that at best marriage is to be tolerated. Coping is the most they hope for. Into this attitude of mediocrity and complacency comes a God who desires to give life and give it abundantly. This doesn't mean special protection from problems, but it does mean joy, peace, and liberty in the midst of them. Part of His plan for such abundance is the divine relationships through which He works—marriage, the family, and the church.

▼ *Thanks, Heavenly Father, for being a good God!*

RELAX A LITTLE

*Live joyfully with the wife whom you love all
the days of your vain life.* —ECCL. 9:9

$\mathcal{I}$ just love it when David takes a Monday or Friday off,
when we're both able to relax and enjoy one another's
company. It really feels like a holiday to me. We don't
have to plan our day; we don't need to do anything but
enjoy being with each other.

The world tries to convince us that we need to be
doing something all the time. We often fall into the trap
of an overly busy life. When we stop enjoying each
other's company, it's usually a sign we've given over
more of ourselves than is healthy for our growth as a
couple. How can we feel romantic or get to know one
another on a deeper emotional level unless we make
time to enjoy each other, alone, without the kids or
others around?

▼ *Lord, help me to stay out of the world's trap of the
tyranny of the urgent and remember to take time to
relax.*

ENJOYMENT—SEIZE THE MOMENT

Therefore, as we have opportunity, let us do good to all.
—GAL. 6:10

*T*eresa and I often found the "joy of now" being stolen by past disappointments or future anxieties. It was amazing how difficult it was to just deal with the present! Great joy began to come as we worked hard at "seizing" the moment.

Intimacy is developed and deepened as couples seize the daily experiences which draw them together. Intimacy doesn't just "happen" without effort, but neither can it be "programmed" to happen. Couples seem to grow in closeness, for example, as they "encounter" one another spiritually, emotionally, or physically. Such an encounter might be an ecstatic moment of common joy, a tearful sharing of genuine apology, or an affectionate embrace. In these intimate encounters couples learn to deepen their marital closeness.

 Father, might we seize today's opportunities to enjoy You and each other.

THE JOY OF ENJOYING

For we have great joy and consolation in your love.
—PHILEM. 1:7

*M*y wife has an incredible ability to enjoy happy moments. I'll never forget early in our marriage when I got a great job offer and called to tell her about it. She got so excited that she accidentally hung up the phone. I called her back, and she got so excited that she accidentally hung up the phone again.

Birthdays are the same way. She loves them. She blows up five million balloons, hangs up streamers, buys party hats, and does anything else she can think of to make that birthday the best ever.

My wife really celebrates special moments. I get tremendous enjoyment out of watching her savor happy occasions.

Now that her style has rubbed off on me, I celebrate with more joy. Birthdays are more exciting, anniversaries are more meaningful, and holidays are happier. My wife showed me the way.

Thanks, Holly, for showing me how to enjoy things more.

▼ *God, help us as a couple to really enjoy life together.*

YOU'RE FUN TO BE WITH

For the LORD takes pleasure in His people.
—PS. 149:4

*C*hris has meant a lot of different things to me, but one high on the list would have to be that he's my best friend. I just plain enjoy being with him. We laugh at the same things and cry at the same things. We enjoy trying new restaurants, watching old movies, and taking long walks together. We both enjoy reading, sharing an interesting book with one another. We especially enjoy vacations together. I really enjoy the seminars he gives and go every chance I get. I like to hear him speak and am very proud of him. He likes me to be there too. We enjoy discussing afterward how he did, who all was there, and any suggestions on material.

Are you your spouse's biggest fan? Do you enjoy each other's company? That's what God wants for you.

▼ *Dear God, help me to focus on my spouse and experience a special joy when we are together.*

ENJOYING EACH OTHER'S COMPANY

My times are in Your hand.
—PS. 31:15

*T*ime has only three tenses—past, present, and future—and intimacy is experienced only in the present. Living in the present is difficult, but it's essential for experiencing intimacy and abundance. The present is all we really have to enjoy!

We encourage couples with several suggestions for enjoying each other in the present, First, talk about common interests— *"Can you think of some common interests for us to work on developing?"* Second, communicate your enjoyment— *"I'm not sure I've ever told you, but your friendship is extremely important to me; I enjoy you so much."* Third, discuss your friendship— *"What are some ways we can deepen our friendship?"*

We've also found it helpful to review with couples a return to some "first loves." Recall some of the activities you enjoyed during courtship that were particularly meaningful to your spouse; surprise each other by returning to some of these. Review your hobbies and pastimes to make sure your spouse is not being excluded; include them next time—hunting, golf, fishing, shopping, tennis, walking, etc. Plan times to sit and talk; go for walks; have a date; get away for an overnight trip. A true friend makes time for a friend.

▼ *Teach us, Father, to seize the enjoyment of today!*

ENTREATY—TO BESEECH ANOTHER WITH EXHORTATION, COMFORT, OR CARE

I, therefore, . . . beseech you to walk worthy of the calling with which you were called.
—EPH. 4:1

*C*aring entreaty helps give purpose and passion to life. It's easy to fall into the barrenness of a busy life, faithfully addressing the tyranny of the urgent while the truly significant goes unnoticed. Caring entreaty brings me back to external reality. Life is short, people are eternal, and I can make a difference in their lives!

Teresa seems to have a special sense about the children's needs for time and attention. As the tyranny of busy schedules begins to take its toll on family closeness, she seems to sense the need to reconnect. Her loving entreaty maintains our family priority. "Honey, I think it might be important to plan some relaxing family time . . . everyone seems to be needing it." In a loving way, I've been reminded about what really matters.

▼ *Father, keep me approachable, easy to entreat.*

A CRY FOR HELP

*Therefore I exhort first of all that
supplications, prayers . . . be made for all.*
—1 TIM. 2:1

There's a significant urgency about "entreaty." It might be shared during an evening of quiet reflection or during a private time over dinner. Entreaty might be made over seeing a partner slip away from treasured goals or over the burden of a child missing special time with Mom or Dad. Entreaty says, "I care about you and about priorities that I know are important to you." I care too much to let you miss out on these important priorities. Entreaty is founded on mutual understanding and a trusting vulnerability to share the truth in love.

"Sweetheart, I'm overwhelmed this morning by all that's in front of me. Could we pray together before you go to work?" Such an entreaty is Teresa's loving way to remind me: "I need you to notice and appreciate my struggles, supporting me with your prayer and attention." Her loving entreaty touches in me a "need to be needed." It's a beautiful win-win situation.

▼ *Lord, keep me open and sensitive to my loved ones'
cries for help.*

I NEED YOU!

*He received his entreaty, heard his
supplication.* —1 CHRON. 33:13

I had been feeling lonely for several days due to
David's coming home later and later. After he was home
I knew how tired he was, so I pretty much left him
alone. Lack of intimacy, loneliness, and feeling second
place were taking their toll. If I'd approached David
with, "I'm sick and tired of you being late. Why can't
you ever come home on time?" it wouldn't produce a
desire to change.

One Thursday evening we were in bed when I
reached over and touched him. I looked at him and
said, "I've been really feeling lonely lately. I'll be glad
when we can spend some quality time together." With
the focus on me, he didn't feel defensive. He realized
how busy he'd been and he wanted to correct his
schedule. He took that Monday off to spend with me.
That really made me feel special. My vulnerability in
sharing my need was the tool God could use to convict
David of the need to change.

▼ *Father, thank You for knowing my need and for a
husband who hears You.*

ENTREATY

"Nor do we know what to do, but our eyes are upon You." —2 CHRON. 20:12

I think we should save more money for our children's education." "I think we should pay off our debts." Marriage decisions abound. "I don't like the church we're attending." "I love our church." Marriage oneness is tested. 'I can't go on like this!'" "Things aren't nearly that bad." Marriage intimacy is lost. Life is a series of daily decisions, "fork in the road" decisions with the potential for harmony or discord. A beginning place is to *entreat* the Lord together, acknowledging our need and desire for divine direction.

Notice the "oneness" among the people in this Scripture passage. "We know not what to do." We're united in not having answers! That's the start of oneness. "But our eyes are upon You." We're united in looking to God for wisdom and direction. Oneness can proceed. Together we trust a good God to grant a "peace that passes all understanding."

▼ *Father, unite our hearts in entreaty for Your wisdom and direction. We know not what to do.*

I URGE YOU TO CONSIDER THIS

Now we exhort you, brethren.
—1 THESS. 5:14

*H*ave you ever known anyone so concerned about an issue that they *urged* you to do something about it. To them, the issue was so critically important that just asking you to do something or mildly pleading with you wasn't enough.

There are issues like that in marriage. When I was going through some tough emotional struggles, Holly urged me to go get some counseling. Being a psychologist, I felt an unfortunate sense of threat about going to counseling because, after all, a counselor is supposed to be perfectly healthy. Holly was so concerned about my pain that she urged me to get counseling.

I'm glad to say I went, and it helped me. But I trace it back to her caring enough to urge me to go.

When a situation in marriage is serious enough to require much more than a simple "Please" or "I hope you will," we need to urge the other person to take a course of action or to be urged to take a course of action. When someone is urging you about something, make sure you listen to what they say. The fact that they are urging you about it means they see it with utmost seriousness.

▼ *God, help us to know when to urge our spouses about something. Help us not urge them about small things.*

DON'T MISS OUT

Now we exhort you, brethren, warn those who are unruly, comfort the fainthearted, uphold all the weak, be patient with all.
—1 THESS. 5:14

$\mathcal{D}$addy, will you play with me?" The question was fine. It was her husband's response lately, that concerned Janet. "No, honey, I'm too busy. Maybe later." But of course later never came. And another precious day would be lost without time spent with his kids. Didn't her husband see what a bad pattern he was starting to get into? Janet felt compelled to bring it to his attention. "Honey, I'm really concerned about you're not spending time with the kids. They seem to be taking a back seat to other things. What do you think?" Bill replied, "I think you're right. I'm feel as if I'm just filling my time with more things I need to get done. I want to get back on the right track with my family. Any suggestions?" Janet answered, "Why don't you plan on spending thirty minutes to an hour each night playing with the kids?" You could do different things each night, reading, playing outside, or crafts. Maybe you could set aside one night a month as special for each child. That's an idea to start with."

Janet didn't want her husband to look back at his life with regret. She lovingly pointed out that relationships bring joy and satisfaction. Bill had been settling for less.

▼ *Father, help me to love my spouse enough to speak out when I see something wrong. Show them, through me, that You want them to have more in life.*

ENTREATY FROM SHARED READING AND REFLECTION

He began to entreat Him earnestly.
—MARK 5:10 NASB

*E*ntreating your spouse can be scary. We recommend shared reading as a neutral setting to promote vulnerable exchanges. Teresa and I have benefited from reading together books on communication, parenting, goal setting, and sexual intimacy. As we share ideas, insights, hopes, and fears about a topic, our closeness deepens.

Many of the couples we counsel also have benefited from shared reading followed by a time of reflection. Books or other writings often serve as a neutral third-party source of ideas to help stimulate discussion and interaction. We might encourage couples to take turns picking reading material—this month she may pick a book on marriage communication or childraising; next month he may pick a popular Christian book or a world events magazine. Each partner then reads the selected material—particularly noting items of keen interest. Maybe they take turns reading one chapter at a time, or read aloud to each other. The couple then schedules times of reflection to comment on the reading and share particular items of personal/practical interest. This setting gives couples an opportunity to be more vulnerable about their ideas, desires, and wishes.

 Make me open to the ideas, feelings, and opinions of this special person in my life.

EXALTED—LIFTED UP IN DIGNITY AND RESPECT AS A PERSON OF GREAT WORTH

"And he who humbles himself will be exalted."
—LUKE 14:11

It feels great to have someone view you as a person of "great worth"; to have such a promise of exaltation from the Lord is tremendous. To be valued as important by one's spouse may be the highest exaltation one can receive from another human. Others in work, church, or community may lift me up, but there's no comparison with the impact of "I'm proud of you," from my spouse.

This exaltation might come from a private compliment or public praise. It might come in declining to commit to a child's major request until time for discussion with your spouse. It might come in a tender moment of reflection: "I'm sure glad you're my wife; I love you." Whatever its form, lifting your partner up as a special person is essential for an intimate marriage.

▼ *Let my words and actions exalt the great worth of my spouse.*

MARY'S EXALTATION

"My soul magnifies the Lord."
—LUKE 1:46

In our souls we experience emotions like gratitude, thankfulness, and "wonder." Wonderment must have been at least part of what Mary experienced in her joyful declaration. The mysteries of God's workings are a joyous wonder—even in the spouse He has given! His blessings are endless, many coming through this life partner He has provided.

More and more frequently in these passing years of marriage, I've felt a touching sense of deep gratitude for the life-partner God has given me: a partner who has seen my "darker side" and still accepts me; a partner with strengths to lovingly balance my weaknesses; a partner with whom I'd rather just sit quietly than to experience any of life's thrills without her; a partner who thinks of me, gives to me, cares about me; a partner my God has given me.

▼ *My soul magnifies the Lord.*

BUILD UP YOUR SPOUSE

Edify one another.
—1 THESS. 5:11

I didn't realize how often I'd undermined David's authority in the home until the evening we were going out with some friends and I saw myself in another wife.

The husband had grounded their son and had already given him instructions on what he was and wasn't allowed to do. The mother started to add to the father's instructions with the father there. She conveyed the message, "Your father's instructions weren't sufficient, so here are the ones you're to abide by."

I'm to be a living example of how the father is to be exalted in the home. How I exalt David in the position of authority in the home will be caught by my children.

▼ *God, help me be a good example to those around me.*

EXALTATION THROUGH PRIORITY TIME

There is an appointed time for everything.
—ECCL. 3:1

*T*eresa and I have found if you don't plan time for your marriage, the tyranny of every other thing will destroy it. For more than ten years, we have met for lunch once a week. We each made the time a priority, avoiding conflicts and distractions as much as possible. We did our family "calendaring" together for the next week including social engagements, kids' activities and nights for working late. We noticed an almost immediate benefit just from both of us knowing ahead of time what our plans were; we were less irritated and had less conflict.

After getting a grip on the urgent things in our schedule, we used our weekly meetings to begin eliminating activities of a lesser priority and adding items like a weekly date together and periodic weekend get-aways. One guideline we began to use in our time commitments was that neither would commit to an activity that would affect us both until we discussed it together. With our schedules better under control and more fun couple activities on our calendar, we began to use our time to visit more about goal-setting and dreams for the future. Appreciative reflections and caring words came more frequently. We changed our meeting times from Thursday to Saturdays some time back but the benefits are so great that staff meetings are here to stay!

 Lord, might there be an exaltation of my spouse through the priority of my time.

HAPPY BIRTHDAY

> *In Your hand is power and*
> *might;*
> *In your hand it is to make great*
> *And to give strength to all.*
> —1 CHRON. 29:12

*M*y thirty-fourth birthday was nearing, and I wasn't particularly pleased. I felt old and did a pretty good job of letting anyone within earshot know. Holly did her best to counter my complaints, but it didn't help. I was determined to have a pity party about the unfairness of getting older.

I assumed Holly and I would just go out for dinner together to celebrate. As we headed toward our table I looked up and saw eight of our closest friends sitting there. Holly had secretly asked them to come celebrate my birthday.

That really lifted my spirits. Holly had gone to a lot of trouble to let me know that I was a person of great value. She turned what I was bent on making an unpleasant birthday into one of the best I've ever had. I felt exalted that day, like a king. It is a nice feeling, one we all need every so often.

When was the last time you exalted your spouse? Pick out one day in the next month and make your spouse king/queen for a day.

▼ *God, help me to lift my spouse up and show him/her the person of great value that he/she is.*

I'M WALKING ON AIR

An excellent wife is the crown of her husband.
                                            —PROV. 12:4

*H*ave you ever overheard your spouse brag to someone about you? That happened to me the other day. Chris was on the phone with a friend. I had just finished putting the kids to bed and walked into the bedroom where he was. His back was to me. All of a sudden I heard him say my name, so naturally my ears pricked up. He was telling his friend what a great attitude I'd had over the delay of our house. We were building a house and, for various reasons, it had gone over completion time by several months. He went on to say how appreciative he was that I hadn't spent my time complaining but had sought instead to make the best out of current living arrangements, what a help that had been to his peace of mind. That compliment meant so much to me because I knew it was from his heart. Chris was lifting me up to his friend as a wife of great value. And believe me, because of hearing what I did, I'm especially careful to continue being a good sport about the house. I'd hate for him to have to change his mind.

▼ *Lord, help me to lift up my spouse as valuable, to share my thankfulness for my spouse with others.*

20 WAYS TO EXALT YOUR SPOUSE

*So speak and so do as those who will be
judged by the law of liberty*
—JAMES 2:12

Sandy and Rod desired enrichment in their marriage.
Each was extremely reserved, giving poor eye contact
and very closed body language. Each cared deeply for
the other, but rarely expressed it.

After two sessions to address unresolved hurt within
the relationship, we tackled their expressiveness. I gave
them each a list of 20 ways to exalt each other.

• You're Incredible • You're Fantastic • You're
Beautiful • You're Unique • You're Precious
• You're Important • You're Sensational • You're
Exciting • You're a Good Listener • You're Special to
Me • You're a Good Friend • You're Important
• You Mean a Lot to Me • You Make Me Happy
• You Make Me Laugh • You Brighten My Day • You
Mean the World to Me • You're a Joy • You're Won-
derful • You're the Best

They were to pick one of the exaltations that expressed their inner feeling, then hold hands, look each
other in the eye, and verbalize it. It was difficult for
them, but as Rod softly said, "You mean a lot to me,"
and Sandy replied, "You're special to me," tears flowed
and they were closer to their goal of enrichment.

 *Open my mouth that I might speak words that exalt
this special person.*

EXHORTATION—URGING TOWARD POSITIVE CONDUCT AND DECISION-MAKING

Be ready in season and out of season. . . .
Exhort, with all longsuffering and teaching.
—2 TIM. 4:2

*T*eresa and I learned early in marriage how *not* to live married life. One of these fateful lessons came from my trying to "preach" at Teresa. I took the role of exhorter, quoting verses to tell her how she ought to live. But it didn't work.

I learned about exhortation with longsuffering from looking at the Spirit's work in my life. He prompts and urges me toward Christlikeness, but always with patience. He doesn't expect me to get it perfect the first time, whatever it is—witnessing, confession, prayer. He doesn't try to motivate me through fear of His rejection. No wonder His prompting is so easily received: no demands for perfection; no fear of rejection.

When I tried this at home, Teresa and I grew together and became more unified. Gradually we began to read Scripture together, and even had quiet times and memorized a few verses together.

▼ *Father, keep me patient in my confidence that You produce Christlikeness, not me!*

WHAT AUTHORITY?

*Speak these things; exhort . . . with all
authorty.*   —TITUS 2:15

*T*rue exhortation is grounded in His authority—the
Scriptures. Urging my opinions or advice upon my
spouse is not exhortation. It might be advice-giving or
nagging, but not exhortation. Exhortation with all authority implies time spent in the Scriptures becoming
familiar with "the authority." "These things" that are to
be the content of Titus' urging were things which the
Holy Spirit had inspired Paul to write.

Each relationship and each home looks to some authority for its direction and standards. Homes are built
upon the solid rock or upon sinking sand:

> *The grass withers, the flower fades,*
> *But the word of our God stands forever.*
>   *(Isa. 40:8)*

Scripture is our firm and eternal foundation. Many a
time I've left the house confused, needing direction or
answers. What a joy it is to have a scriptural insight or
principle come to mind during drive times, and what a
blessed joy to share it with my wife.

▼ *Thanks, Father, for the unshakable foundation from
Your word.*

GENTLE WORDS

*What do you want? Shall I come to you with
a rod, or in love and a spirit of gentleness?*
—1 COR. 4:21

*W*eight control is a constant battle for me. I can become so wrapped up in trying to control my weight that I can lose balance in my thinking. I become compulsive or overly perfectionistic.

It has been so nice to be able to talk my feelings over with David. I've been able to tell David my plan for the day and ask him to pray for me. Sometimes, because of my compulsiveness or the perfectionism, David needs to exhort me to rethink my plans. David's exhortation always comes with patience and gentleness. I've never felt put down or belittled, and I know David would never use my weakness to tease or hurt me in any way.

▼ *Father, You can make us feel better about ourselves
even when we've blown it.*

EXHORTATION IN THE BEDROOM

> *On my bed night after night I sought him*
> *Whom my soul loves.*
> **—SONG 3:1 NASB**

$\mathcal{A}$my and Greg fought constantly over their sexual intimacy. According to Amy, every night when the kids were in bed, Greg would begin to "exhort" her about her lack of sexual desire. The result? Her lack of sexual desire grew worse!

We suggested they move these discussions out of the bedroom to a quiet time while relaxing. There they were able to discuss their sexual relationship in a positive, pro-active manner, rather than in a reactive way.

Amy and Greg made great progress with this approach. They planned times together sexually, which kept one of them from looking forward to sex all day, only to find that there was no mutual desire. They also learned to part in the morning with tender touches and expressions of, "I'd sure like to be together with you tonight—let's plan on it!" And they even began to set aside a night alone without kids, friends, or other distractions for some unhurried lovemaking.

▼ *Might our physical intimacy be a testimony of God's plan for abundant marriage.*

GET A PICTURE OF THIS

*And let us consider one another in order to
stir up love and good works.*
—HEB. 10:24

A number of years ago, I was in the habit of not
being particularly discriminating about what motion
pictures I would and wouldn't see. My sensitivity to vio-
lence and foul language in films had lessened without
my noticing, and it had become common for me to go
see popular, high-body-count movies with foul language
every other sentence.

In her desire to grow closer to God, Holly became
convicted about the same problem in her own life; and
she made a commitment to God not to see these films
anymore. At first, I felt critical. After all, many of our
Christian friends were seeing these films.

Then, God convicted me. He showed me that Holly
was right. The films were putting into our minds the
ideas and images that God did not want us to have.

I tell you this story just to say that Holly led the way
on this issue by setting a loving, nonpreachy example.
That example was her way of exhorting me toward
Christlike conduct. What I first criticized, I now praise.
She was right; I wasn't. She stood firm in a loving manner while I rationalized and argued. She did what God
wanted her to until He could bring her husband
around.

▼ *God, help me, through example, to challenge my
spouse to Christlike conduct.*

TRUTH OR CONSEQUENCES

For God did not call us to uncleanness, but in holiness.
—1 THESS. 4:7

*J*im dominated every conversation he was in, no matter who he was talking to or what the topic was.

People at church dreaded seeing him come their direction. Patty, his wife, could see it in their eyes. Once she even saw a couple turn right around in midstep and walk the other way. It was heartbreaking to watch, but she just couldn't bring herself to tell him the truth.

One day, Patty read in the Bible that sharing the truth with others was a sign of true love. So she prayed God would provide just the right time to share with Jim his blind spot. Out of the blue, her husband started telling her about his frustration with beginning a men's Bible study. He couldn't get anyone interested.

Patty drew in a deep breath, squared her shoulders, and said, "Jim, I want to share something with you that may be hard to hear. I think one of the reasons you're having trouble recruiting people may be that you tend to dominate conversations." He looked at her in stunned silence; then tears began to roll down his cheeks. In muffled tones, he replied, "I know I talk a lot. Patty, no one has ever had the courage to tell me to my face. It hurts, but I know you're right. I might have never really known if you hadn't."

▼ *God, please help me to honestly and lovingly help my spouse grow, and help me to be open to what my spouse needs to tell me.*

COMMON EXHORTATIONS

*And when [Paul] had gone through those
districts and had given them much
exhortation, he came to Greece.*
—ACTS 20:2 NASB

*C*ouples often come to counseling wanting behavioral suggestions on what to do. While underlying issues need to be dealt with, sooner or later, practical suggestions will be made. Often it's our counseling role to exhort couples to face issues they've been reluctant to face to heal the past and enjoy the present.

A common encouragement we give is to *heal hurts quickly*. Occasional misunderstandings, irritations, and impatient words are inevitable in close relationships; the critical issue is healing hurts through genuine apology and forgiveness (see James 5:16). A good goal is not to let the sun go down on anger; either person should feel free to bring up an unresolved hurt, knowing they'll be heard and cared for.

A second area of common exhortation relates to initiative. Frequently each partner waits for the other so we exhort each to *initiate meeting needs*. Don't wait on your spouse to move first; plan a date, send an appreciative note, begin marriage "staff" meetings. Our counseling goals often focus on each partner gaining an inner freedom to then begin to initiate giving to the other. This initiative in mutual giving is characteristic of maturity, abundance, and intimacy.

▼ *Encourage us with the urgency of being a doer of the Word.*

FORGIVENESS—TO CANCEL OUT OR "RELEASE" WRONGS COMMITTED AND BESTOW INSTEAD UNCONDITIONAL FAVOR

Forgiving one another as God in Christ forgave you.
—EPH. 4:32

*T*o cancel out a debt is an accounting reference to its being paid in full. That's what Calvary did—for me and everyone who has sinned against me. God the Father by His Son's death has stamped "Paid in Full" across every sin ledger. If only each person would receive this gift and then share this same forgiveness with others, marriages would be very different; families would become places of soothing refuge.

Often in our counseling sessions we speak of the stewardship of forgiveness. Forgiveness is first received from God and then shared with others. In a sense, forgiveness is a divine gift to be shared. Marriages and families that keep this divine forgiveness in circulation experience an atmosphere of security and healing.

▼ *Thanks, Father, for the unspeakable glory of Your forgiveness.*

FORGIVENESS—A DIVINE REALITY

*Through this Man is preached to you the
forgivness of sins.*   —ACTS 13:38

$\mathscr{P}$roclamation of the good news is what my Christian testimony is all about. Maybe there's no more powerful vehicle of proclamation than forgiving others as I have been forgiven. Forgiveness is a divine reality that I first must receive from my Creator, then find myself prompted by His spirit to share. Maybe one of my strongest testimonies is that I live in harmony with my spouse; the sun doesn't go down on our anger; no root of bitterness springs up between us. Maybe this is part of God's intended testimony from marriage.

We often tell Christian couples as they begin to complete their marriage intimacy "treatment plan" to begin expecting God to use them to encourage others. Intimate marriages, characterized by forgiving hearts, are a great lighthouse to the world. There's a special attractiveness about an intimate marriage that draws others to Christ.

▼ *If He is lifted up, He will draw us unto Him.*

FINISHED BUSINESS

Who is this who even forgives sins?
—LUKE 7:49

$\mathcal{D}$avid has always said I've been a person who could easily forgive. I believe that to be true, but I didn't realize I was only partially working through the forgiveness.

In the Greek *forgiveness* means "to release." When I forgave, I was releasing the person and the action, but I was failing to release my pain. I forgave out of my will, but I still felt hurt later. I chose to forgive again, but still experienced pain. I wasn't dealing with the pain associated with the hurt. I still had unhealed emotions. Forgiveness is dealing with the person, the action, and the emotion behind the action.

Forgiveness can't be conditional. We can't withhold our forgiveness because we know they'll do it again. Only God can know, and He's already forgiven us for the past, present, and future. How, then, can we withhold forgiveness?

▼ *Father, You know every day of my future and You still chose me.*

FORGIVENESS FREES ME FOR ACCEPTANCE

*Forgiving one another, just as God in Christ
also forgave you.* —EPH. 4:32

*J*im and Ellen wanted more than just to know each was loved by the other; they wanted to feel it! For years they had fulfilled their responsibilities, working hard and complaining little. In counseling it became clear that over the years, each would encounter the other's irritable rough edges, reject the other in some way, but quietly avoid dealing with their issues. A classic example was Jim's driving.

Jim drove the family to church each Sunday, never taking the same route, oblivious to Ellen's need to be on time for choir. After repeated Sunday morning conflicts, Ellen decided to take her own car and leave early, but she left angry at Jim's lack of understanding and support. Jim began coming to church later and later each Sunday, angry over Ellen's independence and rejection. They had sustained this and countless other painful coping strategies for eight years until they began to feel emotionally numb.

In our counseling sessions, we identified and healed hurts as anger was forgiven. Their forgiveness of each other prompted their acceptance of each other's needs. Jim accepted Ellen's need to be on time for choir, and Ellen accepted Jim's relaxed, daydreaming drive to church with contentment rather than criticism. Soon their feelings of love were rekindled.

 Search me, Father, for any root of bitterness that holds me captive; free me from my anger.

"IT'S FORGIVEN"

*Even as Christ forgave you, so you also
must do.*   —COL. 3:13

*D*id you know that January is named after the Roman god Janus? He had two faces, one looking back and one looking forward. January is the month when we take time to do both as well—take a look back to learn from the previous year and take a look forward to make things better.

Building marital intimacy can also involve doing both, but only properly and for the right reasons. Many couples look back to unearth painful events for the purpose of punishing each other. Spouses who do that to each other will look to the future with bitterness and hopelessness.

Husbands and wives need to look back to learn from the past. And, as hard as it is to do, we need to forgive our spouses for wrongs they have done to us so that we don't carry anger and resentment into each day. Using the past that way, we are better able to look ahead to the future with anticipation.

God desires that we forgive our spouses for how they have wronged us in the past and that we look forward with anticipation to how He will make our marriages a place of joy in the future.

▼ *God, please help me use our marital past as a learning experience, a chance to forgive, and a springboard into an enjoyable, growing future.*

A NEW BEGINNING

If you have anything against anyone, forgive him, so that your Father in heaven may also forgive you your trespasses.
—MARK 11:25

Forgiving someone for a wrong is not easy. Yet life can't be lived to its fullest extent if we harbor unforgiveness toward others, especially our spouses.

In order to forgive your spouse for wrongdoing, you need to see things as God does. He knows that the sin of your spouse is a reflection of who he/she is inside and not you. God wants us to step inside their shoes and feel their pain as well. If you can, you will see a weak and hurting soul. God wants us to respond in holy empathy and forgiveness. Instead of being an instrument of destruction, sinfully responding to the sin, we can let God use us as an instrument of healing.

Forgiveness is easier to talk about than to do. Yet few things are more burdensome than going through life with an unforgiving spirit, especially in marriage.

Let your spouse off the hook because God did that for you when you didn't deserve it.

▼ *God, please help me forgive my spouse for wrongs, even when the wrongdoing persists. Help me to remember that You did that for me.*

HEALING MARITAL HURTS

Let all bitterness, wrath, anger, clamor, and
evil speaking be put away from you . . .
forgiving one another. —EPH. 4:31–32

$\mathcal{A}$s I have worked through the forgiveness process in my relationship with Teresa, I have found several significant issues.

First, hurting Teresa also hurts God—and needs His forgiveness (1 John 1:9). It's sobering to realize that my selfishness or unloving attitude or abusive/demeaning words were exactly why Christ died for me! This Godly sorrow brings change within me. Second, "I was wrong" is much better than "I am sorry," since *wrong* tends to convey more responsibility/remorse/repentance. The word *confess* means to "agree with" God, and God says these things are wrong. Third, it seemed to bring closure to the issue for me to ask "Will you forgive me?" after I've come to understand Teresa's hurt. The vulnerability of this question conveys important humility as well as challenges Teresa with her decision to forgive. Last, Teresa and I have found that forgiveness is a choice—not a feeling! To put away anger, wrath, and bitterness and forgive each other is a command to choose to forgive. It helps us to seal this choice by verbalizing our forgiveness—"I forgive you."

▼ *Lord, lead us alone with You often to seek Your forgiveness, and then together for confession and forgiveness.*

FREEDOM—LIBERTY FROM FEAR AND OBLIGATION

[Act] as free, as bondservants of God.
—1 PET. 2:16

$\mathcal{A}$ free man is under no obligation and is not motivated by fear; such is the Christian's heritage. Grace frees me from the bondage of performance; security in Christ frees me from fear of His judgment or rejection. Because of the gift of such love, I now have something to share with others, beginning with my spouse. I can share grace and not fear, acceptance and not rejection.

In counseling we see too many couples who live in fear: fear of being rejected, fear of divorce, fear of abandonment. It's not uncommon to find one spouse being controlled by the other's threats of leaving. The threat may have been spoken only once early in the marriage or may be repetitive. The pain of such a threat is great, and the resultant fear is enormous. Repentance and confession are needed to free the marriage of any such fear. Reassurances are often needed, and repeating wedding vows might be recommended. An atmosphere of freedom is worth the investment.

▼ *Perfect love casts out all fear.*

SET FREE!

*Stand fast . . . in the liberty by which Christ
has made us free.*
                                        —GAL. 5:1

*G*od's plan in freeing me from the penalty of my sin
was that I might enjoy still more freedom! There will be
a future freedom from the presence of pain and sin, but
just as certain is the promise of *present* freedom, freedom from fleshly control and selfish preoccupation,
freedom for the life *I now* live. A special part of God's
abundance for the "here and now" is the freedom to
love and be loved by one's partner.

Teresa and I have come to find a great blessing in
learning to allow each other to relax. At times one of us
has a schedule so hectic relaxing doesn't seem like an
option. Then the spouse has a unique ministry, giving
the other "permission" to relax and enjoy life. Teresa
has often said, "I've noticed how hard you've been
working lately, and I think *we* would enjoy some quiet
time just for us." She helps reorient my priorities and
ministers freedom to me.

▼ *Thanks, Father, for filling our marriage with
freedom.*

OUR THREE KIDS

But I want you to be free from concern.
—1 COR. 7:32 NASB

𝒢od desires for children to bring the family together as a whole unit, for the husband and wife to be united in the rearing of their children.

The biggest challenge I had with our children was trusting David's decisions. I felt I knew the most about child raising because I'd been the one doing most of it. (David was frequently away for business.)

God showed me I had to release my children and my husband to Him. God had to bring unity in our marriage first, then we had the freedom to raise our kids with the oneness God desires.

Our children are almost grown. We honestly like and enjoy being with our kids. I know in my heart if I'd not trusted God with my husband and my kids our lives would be very different today.

▼ *Father, You have filled our quiver with three beautiful arrows.*

FREEDOM TO ACCEPT ME SPIRITUALLY

Where the Spirit of the Lord is, there is liberty.
                                    —2 COR. 3:17

$\mathscr{D}$uring a counseling session, Russell and Ann expressed embarrassment and frustration over how little they shared spiritually. Their spiritual oneness consisted of weekly attendance in the same church pew, singing from the same hymnal. They had come from different Protestant backgrounds, and rather than risk controversy or rejection, they avoided discussing anything "spiritual." I suggested a homework assignment. Russell and Ann were to visit quietly for a few minutes before going to sleep. After visiting, they were to hold hands and pray silently together for a minute or two. They were then to squeeze hands affectionately and go to sleep. The couple agreed to try it.

At our next session they reported a special closeness and wanted to make these talk-prayer times a part of their evening bedtime routine. Intimacy doesn't happen without effort, but neither can it be "programmed." Why not try this talk-prayer experiment with your spouse?

▼ *Lord, might Your purpose of oneness find its way into the depths of our spiritual journey together.*

FREEDOM TO BE DIFFERENT

Christ has made us free.
—GAL. 5:1

I like vanilla ice cream; Holly likes chocolate. I squeeze the toothpaste from the end; she squeezes it in the middle. I'm melancholic; she's sanguine.

Amazing, isn't it, how different we can be from our spouses. Sad, though, that instead of accepting these differences we often try to force our style on our spouses as "the correct way" to do or be.

One of the toughest challenges in marriage involves accepting and supporting our spouses' freedom. God made them unique. He wants us to support their freedom to like chocolate ice cream, squeeze the toothpaste in the middle, be whatever temperament they are, and prefer Italian food.

So the next time you are tempted to take the old "You should think and act just like me" attitude in your marriage, stop and think about it. Can you let your spouse be who (s)he is?

▼ *God, please help me support my spouse's freedom to be who (s)he is.*

FREE TO BE YOU AND ME

Freely you have received, freely give.
—MATT. 10:8

I'm a spender; he's a saver.
I'm lax on discipline; he's very disciplined.
I'm less than neat; he's obsessively so.
I'm passive; he's aggressive.
I'm a feeler; he's a thinker.

𝒟o you have a marriage like this? Those differences probably attracted you to each other in the first place, but later they can help drive you apart.

I think God brings people who are different together for a purpose. It stretches us as human beings, and we become more flexible.

In Christ, we have the freedom to be different and not feel guilty! Our personal differences keep life interesting and exciting. Yet, sadly, we often turn personal differences into strychnine.

God wants us to grow and uses our differences in marriage to help us accomplish that. Strange as it may sound, we can thank Him for how different we are as spouses.

▼ *Lord, thank You for our freedom in Christ to be unique. Help us respect our spouse's freedom and to use differences to grow in maturity.*

FREEDOM IN THE BEDROOM

*May he kiss me with the kisses of
his mouth!
For your love is better than wine.*
—SONG 1:2 NASB

$\mathcal{C}$ouples often come for counsel complaining of sexual difficulties. Why is there so little interest? Why do I not look forward to being together sexually?

Physical oneness is a significant third of the marital relationship. During one of your talk times, discuss typical hindrances.

Resentment and romance don't go together. Letting the sun go down on your hurts will let anger quench romance and affection—heal your hurts as they inevitably happen. The bedroom is the worst place to discuss changes you'd like in your sexual routine; wait until you are relaxed and close and then share. Touching only when it leads to sex also develops resentment. Increase your nonsexual touching.

Another major hindrance is the sexual guessing game. Assuming your spouse knows how to sexually stimulate you and then being angry when he or she doesn't is a common trap. Break this cycle by taking turns switching roles. Make love to your spouse exactly the way you'd most enjoy having him or her make love to you. Then reverse the process. Remove boredom by changing routines—locations, time of day, dress, positions, who initiates, and so on. Talk more to each other during your sexual times together—share feelings, desires, and excitement.

 Thanks, Father, for Your plan for our abundant intimacy.

GENTLENESS—THE "SWEET REASONABLENESS" OF KIND, GOOD-NATURED CARING

Blessed are the meek,
For they shall inherit the earth.
—MATT. 5:5

Gentleness is no doubt what the children felt as Jesus blessed them after the disciples' rebuke. Even though they had little to "contribute," the children felt cared for. Their Creator saw great worth in them. For a gentle, caring response, such worth was enough. That's the way it is in marriage—the inherent worth and value of my spouse as declared by our Savior prompts my gentle and caring response.

Most of the important things in life can't be *seen!* You can't see God, or love; you can't see intimacy or care. But each one is very important. Gentle caring seems to flow from a heart warmed by the worth of another human being, a human being special to God and to me.

▼ *Thanks, Father, for the immeasurable worth we see declared at Calvary.*

A GENTLE SAVIOR

Take My yoke upon you . . . for I am gentle.
—MATT. 11:29

$\mathcal{T}$he Gospel writers used various adjectives to describe the Messiah: filled with grace, compassionate, loving. Christ himself used the words *gentle* and *humble!* Gentleness is often not valued today. Getting my own way and asserting my rights seem to be more in vogue, but not very Christlike. Gentleness always conveys tenderness and warmth; it doesn't call attention to itself, but others feel it.

In our high-tech society, interpersonal skill is often lacking. We often work with couples on tone of voice, facial expression, eye contact, nonsexual touching, and emotional openness—all of which contribute to gentleness. We might work on sharing confessions to heal resentments and giving reassurances to lessen fears. It's exciting to see couples come to enjoy the closeness of gentle caring.

▼ *Teach me Your gentleness, O Lord.*

CRUDE AND RUDE

A soft answer turns away wrath.
—PROV. 15:1

Speaking with a gentle voice hasn't been one of my strong points. I could be gentle in touching, but my words were not always gentle. My abruptness hurt David and the kids. David called me rude and crude in our early years of marriage and I laughed. My kids were often wounded by my words when I corrected them harshly, instead of gently. As they got older, the kids teased me over the way I said things, and the teasing hurt only because I knew they were right. Seeing myself through my family's eyes produced in me a desire to change. I didn't want to come across as hard or overbearing. I know I respond quicker to a gentle, soft voice than one that is hard and harsh.

▼ *Lord, as You show me through my family what I need to change, help me receive it.*

MIRACLES FROM A GENTLE ANSWER

A gentle answer turns away wrath.
—PROV. 15:1 NASB

*F*ourteen hours after leaving home at daybreak, I drove home, angry about people's incompetencies that had unnecessarily prolonged my day. *If only everyone was like me, we wouldn't have such mix-ups,* I fumed to myself.

It was well after dark when I thundered into the house, my martyrdom running high. Teresa was still up, had graciously reheated dinner, and greeted me warmly. "Honey, you look like you had a really hard day." "Yeah, if you'd had the day I had, you'd look bad too!" I blurted back. The wound was struck; she stood there hurt, shocked by my insensitive, angry response.

She stood silent for ten seconds that seemed like forever. Then, she spoke with divinely empowered gentleness: "I really can see that you've had a hard day, and I'd like to visit about it if you would. But it feels like you're taking it out on me, and that hurts."

With her gentle answer, the Spirit convicted me. There was only one response His Spirit would allow: "You're right; it was wrong of me to hurt you with my anger. Will you forgive me?"

▼ *Might our marriage be often touched by the convicting work of a gentle word.*

A SOFT ANSWER

Let your gentleness be known to all.
—PHIL. 4:5

They say words can be like punches. When I first heard that statement, it hurt. It hurt because I realized how many punches I have hit Holly with over the years through mean or insensitive words that I have spoken in her direction. The words weren't true, and I didn't mean them, but they were punches nevertheless.

Intimacy can be destroyed by words. I admit to my own considerable contribution to this problem. In marriage we all seem to find it difficult to control our tongues. The ability to do so is one of the cornerstones of achieving intimacy in marriage.

The power of words. How often we forget their power to destroy and their power to uplift.

Thrown any punches lately?

▼ *God, help me to watch what I say to my spouse, to uplift and encourage rather than hurt and damage.*

INNER BEAUTY

*We were gentle among you, just as a . . .
mother cherishes her own children.*
—1 THESS. 2:7

J helped out a friend of mine yesterday. Her husband
was having his wisdom teeth out, and he was pretty apprehensive about it. She arranged for me to keep their
young son so she could give her husband her full attention and energy. Her care to the details of timing and
transportation in planning were meticulous. My friend
wanted things to go as smoothly and comfortably as possible for her husband.

In her gestures and speech, in her whole demeanor,
you could see gentleness. I would hear her kindly encourage her husband and listen to his concerns, never
once putting him down for them. She was at the doctor's
office during the entire surgery, the ultimate way to reassure him. Her responses to her husband's needs
spoke volumes to him.

We all long for gentle concern in the marital relationship. My friend inspired me to be more gentle toward
my husband, largely because I saw how much gentleness meant to the person on the receiving end.

▼ *Lord, help me be gentle toward my spouse in my
attempt to meet his/her needs day by day.*

INVOLVING ALL FIVE SENSES IN GENTLE SEX

My beloved extended his hand . . .
And my feelings were aroused for him.
—SONG 5:4 NASB

*C*hristine and Larry came for help in dealing with sexual intimacy. Christine characterized Larry's foreplay as "mauling" and sex as intolerably rough. The roots of Larry's ineptness were typical: He often felt sexually inadequate, and when he wasn't sure what to do, his anxiety came out in increased roughness.

In working with Christine and Larry, we sought to add more gentleness to their sexual intimacy. Sexual closeness is often enhanced as more of the five senses are involved. We encourage couples to be creative about involving more of their senses.

We encouraged Larry and Christine to involve their sense of sight through soft lighting, intimate sleepwear, undressing each other. Increase touching through body massage, bubble bath, sleepwear fabrics, satin sheets. Involve the taste with soft kisses, fruit drinks, body lotions. Stimulate hearing with pleasant music, sound tracks of surf or nature, soft whispers to each other. And even involve the sense of smell with scented candles, perfumed bath oils and powders, colognes and perfume.

You might find it helpful to take turns initiating and leading in your times of physical intimacy—each experimenting with involving all five senses.

 Thanks, Lord, for Your divine purposes in sexual intimacy.

GRACE—FREELY BESTOWED FAVOR
UPON A VALUED PERSON

*Let no corrupt word proceed out of your
mouth, but what is good for necessary
edification, that it may impart grace to the
hearers.*
—EPH. 4:29

*W*hat a sobering privilege to be a minister of divine
grace through my words. Grace has its origin in heaven
and its fullest demonstration at Calvary. Christ's sacrifice shouts of the Father's bountiful grace toward all of
us. My words can share this boundless love and unconditional acceptance with those around me, beginning
with my spouse.

I still remember Teresa's loving request that I be
more attentive to the bathroom mess I seemed to leave
each morning. Her request was shared in gentleness
and vulnerability, letting me know she would appreciate
any assistance the Lord might prompt me to give. There
was no repetitive nagging, no threat of terrible consequences. She trusted God with the outcome. But her
words ministered grace. I began to *desire* to help; I then
found the *power* to do it! The bathroom has never been
the same since.

 *Thanks, Father, for the privilege of sharing divine
grace through our words.*

GRACE: RECEIVE IT, THEN SHARE IT

Of His fullness, we have all received, and
grace for grace. —JOHN 1:16

$\mathcal{G}$race can only be "received." It can't be earned or deserved. It can't be demanded or claimed as a right. It is a gift, freely given by a giver who has an endless supply. Gratitude is one tell-tale sign of a grace recipient, followed by stewardship and giving. First having received from God makes giving possible; I'm then called upon to give from His boundless supply.

Our approach to marriage counseling is based upon this principle of grace, first needing to *receive* from God, then having something to give or *share*. Couples struggling with forgiving one another might be challenged to explore their own forgiveness by God. Partners in a home with tremendous rejection might be challenged to explore God's acceptance of each believer in order to have acceptance to share with one another.

 God, help me to share with my spouse the grace You've given me.

OUR INHERITANCE

*For the grace of God which was given to you
by Christ Jesus.* —1 COR. 1:4

*H*ave you ever wished for an inheritance? Boy, I have! The closest we've ever come to an inheritance was from the end-of-year unclaimed-money tax and bank records. Each year our paper runs the names of individuals who need to collect their money. I always check to see if our names are listed. Eric, our son's name, made the list. We were so excited! How much was it? Where did it come from? His grandmother had started him a savings account at birth, and we'd forgotten about it. We were excited to collect our free, unearned, and undeserved $28.

Grace is our free, unearned, and undeserved inheritance. We also must, by faith, collect it. Having received our free gift of grace we are then free to be able to share it.

▼ *Father, You've so freely given to meet our every need.*

LIBERTY OR BONDAGE?

My thoughts are not your thoughts.
—ISA. 55:8

*I*n the early years of our marriage, it seemed as if Teresa and I were trying to "whip one another into shape." After all, if we didn't keep the pressure on, the other one might never change! How wrong we were. God had a better way. Accept one another unconditionally and He'll prompt and empower needed changes!

Many couples travel the broad path of performance but its end is destructive. Few couples travel the narrow path of unconditional giving but its end is greatly blessed.

Why should one for whom Christ freely died have to earn my acceptance? Which will it be in your home and marriage—liberty or bondage?

▼ *I'm grateful, Father, for Your ways being wiser than mine.*

GRACE LIBERATES GIVING

Do not turn your freedom into an opportunity for the flesh, but through love serve one another.
                                    —GAL. 5:13 NASB

 For the four years of their marriage, Anthony and Cecelia had fought over the most bizarre issues. She boiled the tea too long and let the bath water run too long before entering the tub. He bounced the baby too high on his knee and didn't secure the diapers well enough.

As we began to explore the underlying issues prompting such behaviors, it became clear that Anthony and Cecelia were "hiders." They were afraid to communicate their longings to each other, so they hid their needs and waged petty wars. Anthony hungered for the verbal affirmation and appreciation he missed from his dad. Cecelia yearned just to sit and talk, be listened to and feel the investment of time in her life she missed in her childhood.

As our counseling progressed, slowly Anthony and Cecelia began moving toward each other as they offered grace to each other. Each began giving without requiring the other to change. Anthony sat and listened to Cecelia *before* she changed the way she made tea. And Cecelia verbally expressed appreciation of Anthony *before* he changed diapers differently.

▼ *Grace removes all conditions from my giving.*

GOLDEN GRACE

*It is good that the hearts be established
by grace.*
                                        —HEB. 13:9

*O*ne of my favorite movies is *On Golden Pond*, a wonderful story about love and commitment between an elderly couple, Norman and Ethel Thayer.

In many ways, I identify with Norman. He is a crotchety man with a fairly cynical attitude. He tends to look on the negative side of things and is pretty bad at emotional intimacy. Ethel is sensitive, loving, and a great encourager. She is full of grace. She reminds me of my wife, Holly.

Watching them interact in the movie was often funny, sometimes painful. Norman's crusty persona is often a source of frustration for Ethel, but she keeps hanging in there with him. He tests her commitment frequently, yet Ethel never fails to meet the test.

They give us a picture of what grace under pressure looks like. I think Holly will be like Ethel Thayer when she is elderly. I hope and pray I am not like Norman.

▼ *God, help me to be gracious toward my spouse no matter how he/she acts.*

A PLACE OF GRACE

It is good for our hearts to be strengthened by grace . . .
—HEB. 13:9

*M*y friend, Lucy, is a stay-at-home mom with three kids. Money is tight, so she keeps an extra child and does occasional part-time work. Even then, the couple can barely pay their bills, especially when an unexpected expense comes along like a car that breaks down or a sick child. Movies and eating out are out of the question. At times it gets discouraging for Lucy.

A friend of Lucy's called to invite her down for a weekend visit, but Lucy would need to pay for transportation. She told her friend it wasn't a good time and that maybe they could do it later. She sadly hung up the phone.

Lucy's husband, Larry, saw how her eyes lit up. He let her know he wanted her to go. He felt they would work it out somehow. Lucy was ecstatic! It was just the right thing to lift her spirits and encourage her.

Larry's willingness to sacrifice for Lucy helped her exchange her sadness for joy. He showed her what grace in action looks like, and it strengthened her.

Marriage is to be a place of grace.

▼ *Lord, help me to do all I can to meet my spouse's needs, letting him/her know how much I value him/her.*

A TRIANGLE OF GRACE

Good stewards of the manifold grace of God.
—1 PET. 4:10 NASB

*M*arriage is one of God's gifts—an extension of His divine grace. In marriage, God has designed a three-dimensional relationship where two people share friendship, fellowship, and passion. We encourage couples to draw a triangle, representing these three dimensions, as a tool for reflection and communication.

Leslie and Jimmy drew their perceived triangles as they answered questions in three important dimensions of their relationship. First, the base of the triangle represented their perception of *friendship*. Does your spouse believe you have fun together as a couple? Share in common interests? Feel emotionally supported by you? Next, they drew a side of the triangle to represent their *fellowship*. Is your spouse secure in the permanence and fidelity of your marriage commitment? In your spiritual closeness? In your common eternal goals? Finally, they drew a side of the triangle that represented their *passion*. Is your spouse comfortable with your touching? Kissing? Is this area a priority to your spouse?

As Leslie and Jimmy shared their drawings, it prompted openness and honesty. Jimmy even apologized as he commented on how short the base of his triangle was, representing how he realized Gretchen was hurting over their lack of friendship.

▼ *Father, enlarge our capacity to enjoy intimacy.*

HAPPINESS—EXPERIENCING "CHEER" AND JOY WITH SOMEONE WHO CARES

Be of good cheer, I have overcome the world.
—JOHN 16:33

*A*ll joy, cheer, and courage have their origin in one ultimate victory: Christ's overcoming all. His having the keys to hell and the grave. The Old Testament saints looked forward to it and the New Testament church looks back upon it. Human history stands divided at this point on Easter morning. It's for this reason that true joy is sensed in the shocking words that morning: He's not here; He's risen! True happiness rests in the certainty that God cares—not just a little, but a lot; not with a small sacrifice on our behalf, but an ultimate sacrifice.

It's always helped me to remain mindful of this type of sacrifice. Teresa seems most to enjoy special time together that has involved a sacrifice on my part. Giving her "leftover" time doesn't make her feel special. Taking a day off just to be with her feels better to her. An out-of-town shopping trip is pure happiness!

▼ *Remind me, Father, of the joy in giving that others might be blessed.*

A HAPPY DRIVE HOME

Is anyone cheerful? Let him sing psalms.
—JAMES 5:13

*P*raise seems to be a logical extension of true happiness, praise to the only good God who desires not to withhold any good thing, praise to the God from whom all blessings flow. Praise flows from a grateful heart, and this gratitude motivates giving to others. This gratefulness keeps marriage a joy and not an obligation. Scripture warns us not to "grow weary while doing good" (Gal. 6:9). When I find myself growing weary in marriage, it's time for a "praise break." Name His benefits one by one. Experience the refreshing joy of a praise-filled heart.

I often use my driving-home time for counting blessings. I try to focus on the blessings of relationship—the joy of being loved by my wife, being accepted by my kids. As I meditate on such blessings, gratitude builds within me; when I arrive home, a grateful heart paves the way for an enjoyable evening.

▼ *Lord, keep me grateful, giving, and expectant.*

IT'S ALL IN YOUR HEAD

By a sad countenance the heart is made better.
—ECCL. 7:3

I'm convinced that my being happy is purely a state of mind. If I'm only seeing what I don't have, how David hasn't changed, then I will be unhappy. Am I being half empty or half full? Many women confess to me that they're just not happy anymore. I always ask if they have unhealed hurts? If I'm carrying unhealed hurts. I'm going to be unhappy. I'll be half empty. On the other hand, if I'm choosing to forgive and let go of my hurts, I'll be able to feel happiness. "Finally, brethren, whatever things are true, whatever things are noble, whatever things are just, whatever things are pure, whatever things are lovely, whatever things are of good report, if there is any virtue and if there is anything praiseworthy—meditate on these things" (Phil. 4:8).

 Father, help us to take our thoughts captive and think only on things that will build up.

HAPPINESS IN THE HERE AND NOW

Trust . . . in the living God, who gives us richly all things to enjoy. —1 TIM. 6:17

*W*e never enjoy being together unless we're on a trip" is a common answer to the counseling question, "What do you enjoy doing together for fun? Getting away from daily routines is important, but can't happiness be found at home? Trips can get expensive, and if home schedules are too hectic, couples often wait too long between trips and "explode" before they can get out of town.

A common pattern in this marriage scene is a seeming inability to live in the *present.* Happiness takes place in the present, not the past or the future.

Commonly I challenge couples to go out alone, with this ground rule: No talking about anything in the past or in the future. You only talk about the *present.* For 90+ percent of couples, this assignment is difficult. "What would we talk about?" I'm often asked. Talk about sunsets and stars, appreciation and love, observations and feelings. Learn to live in the immediacy of "now."

▼ *Carpe diem!* Seize the day!

HAPPY TOGETHER

A merry heart makes a cheerful countenance.
—PROV. 15:13

A musical group called the Turtles had a lot of hits in the late sixties and early seventies, and a favorite of mine was "Happy Together." The lyrics talk about being completely happy with the one you love and how the world is "so very fine" when romantic love is in full bloom.

For me, that song captures some of what we all hope for our marriages—blue skies all around, wanting to be with that person the rest of your life, and anticipating of being together again.

I know all this sounds overly romantic. But I like the song anyway. Even though romantic love gives way to a more mature, sacrificial love, it doesn't hurt to remember the "happy together" feeling that we had when love first flowered. Mature love and romantic love are not mutually exclusive.

▼ *God, help my spouse and me to mature in our love for each other and hang on to that "happy together" feeling.*

IT'S A WONDERFUL LIFE

A happy heart makes a cheerful countenance.
                                    —PROV. 15:13

*W*hen we moved to Austin eight months ago, we thought we'd be living in an apartment three to four months while our home was being built. Because of delays, we're still in the apartment. There have definitely been frustrations.

But it's been a happy time because we concentrated on relationships. Since our belongings have been in storage, most of what we use is rented, donated, or disposable. Basic and simple, more time and less worry.

We've spent lots of time exploring Austin. And Chris and I committed ourselves to time together before we were sucked under again by busy overscheduling. Chris planned his workload to spend a morning a week with me, just having fun. We also try for a date night out every couple of weeks.

Experiencing joy or cheer with your spouse won't often just happen—it demands time and energy.

 Lord, help me to create an atmosphere of joy and cheer with my spouse.

"DATES," COMMON INTERESTS, AND OTHER GOOD TIMES

I have called you friends, for all things that I heard from My Father I have made known to you.
— JOHN 15:15

Friendship requires time together! It's a shallow commitment to desire friendship but never do much together. This is a challenge we give to most couples we see. Closeness is built as memorable, fun times are enjoyed. Couples are encouraged to increase their "giving" to each other in one or more important ways.

During the upcoming week couples would be encouraged to *date again*. Return to some little things you enjoyed while dating—sit together, hold hands, wear favorite perfume, play "your" song, go to a special restaurant. *Develop common interests;* take turns picking something fun to do—sports, hobby, outing, activity, civic or cultural event. Learn to enjoy being together. *Share 30-second phone calls*—"Hi, Honey, I was thinking of you and wanted to call and remind you that I love you and look forward to seeing you tonight." *Initiate-initiate-initiate*—give verbalized love, hugs, touch, appreciation, love notes, and sexual sharing. Give a *welcome home*—notice each other as you arrive home; initiate contact, smile, touch—communicate "I'm glad to see you." Try some of these ideas this week—you might like them!

▼ *Help me to give today toward a happy marriage.*

HARMONY—AN ENVIRONMENT OF PLEASANT ACCEPTANCE AND SECURE LOVE

And He put all things under His feet.
—EPH. 1:22

"It is finished." The battle is over. From Calvary and the empty grave came the keys to peace and harmony. Harmony is now possible between God and humanity. The God-man Christ has spanned the gap caused by my sin, and in Him I can find rest from the pain of guilt and the struggle to perform. Just as God labored six days and then rested, so now also I can enter into His rest through Christ. Harmony floods my soul. In this harmony with my Creator, I am prompted to share peaceable love with those for whom I care.

Too often, though, my inner stress and turmoil spill out on Teresa and the kids. I become impatient or withdrawn and unavailable. At these times divine intervention is needed, time alone to cast my cares upon Him, time for His peace. Now harmony at home is possible.

▼ *Keep me in harmony within . . . and then let me share it.*

HARMONY AT HOME

All of you be of one mind . . . be
tenderhearted, be courteous.
—1 PET. 3:8

*H*armony attracts just as conflict repels. Harmony in relationship frees me from having to be on guard. Create a harmonious home, and partners will want to be there. Create a harmonious family, and children—even teenagers—will want to be there.

My "workaholic" tendencies have often caused Teresa and me conflict. After a decade or so, we began to notice a connection between my work hours and our harmony at home. The more we improved our marriage harmony, the less I worked late. I found myself wanting to hurry home!

Harmony seems to be closely tied to providing an atmosphere where shared feelings are safe. Harmony is related to our "connectedness," rejoicing with those who rejoice, weeping with those who weep. In Christ we're all members of one body. Husband and wife have become one flesh.

▼ *Father, whatever harmony at home is, we need it.*

WHIP AND DRIVE

Better is a dry morsel with quietness,
Than a house full of feasting with strife.
—PROV. 17:1

I know that in the Ferguson home, there is harmony when I am not competing with David for the role of leader. David says I have the gift of taking over, and when I'm in that mode, I "whip and drive." This isn't a compliment!

When I fall into the "whip and drive" mode, I'm feeling insecure. I may be fearful over finances, what's happening with the kids, or what David's not doing.

Disharmony in the home always filters down from the parents to the children. It affects how well we produce in our jobs and the kids in their school. When I share my fears with David and not try to whip and drive, he helps me with my fears, and the harmony in our home is maintained.

▼ *God, when we seek You, we'll have peace and harmony in our home.*

THE VALUE OF HARMONY

For to me, to live is Christ, and to die is gain.
—PHIL. 1:21

$\mathcal{D}$oug and Pam fought constantly over how to raise their children. Should the kids be made to say their nightly prayers? How about making beds and brushing teeth? What TV programs and how many? The list of parenting conflicts was endless, and they presented them for me to referee!

My response shocked them: "In the final analysis it won't matter how you deal with these issues. The main issue is your harmony about the answer!" Having two adult parents in oneness is more important to a child than the "perfect" answer about bedtime, TV, diet, or teeth-brushing. More important than an extra hour in bed is the security of parental harmony, the freedom from anxiety and restlessness over parental conflict.

Talk; compromise; be creative. At all costs, find harmony.

▼ *The gift of harmony to your family is worth the price of death to self.*

DON'T SWEAT THE SMALL STUFF

Be of the same mind toward one another.
—ROM. 12:16

*Y*our spouse leaves the dishes in the sink after promising to clean them up and there is nothing clean to eat on when dinner rolls around. Your spouse is supposed to pick up the dry cleaning and doesn't, leaving you without a much needed article of clothing for an important engagement.

Sound familiar? Small things, really. They don't rank up there with losing a job, a serious illness, or the death of a loved one.

Yet they can seem to be huge, can't they, particularly when you are in a bad mood or had a rough day. We often find ourselves "making mountains out of molehills" in marriage.

Marriage requires seeing events in their proper size. Letting molehills be molehills is part of the hard work of being intimate in marriage.

▼ *God, help me to let molehills be molehills in my marriage.*

ARE WE ON THE SAME PAGE?

*Fulfill my joy by being like-minded, having
the same love, being of one accord, of one
mind.*　　　　　　　　　　　　**—PHIL. 2:2**

*C*arrie really wanted a dining room table and chairs.
For a year, Tom, her husband, had promised her she
could have them, and she was getting angrier by the
day. To motivate Tom and perhaps to get even, she frequently brought up, in front of others, how he was not
taking very good care of them. Tom knew if he wanted
peace in the house he'd have to give in—but that's what
he always did and it never lasted long.

Sound familiar? If not you, don't you know at least
one couple who function like this? One spouse wants
something, a bigger house or a better car and treats the
other spouse pretty unkindly until they get it. The mi-
rage of harmony doesn't last long—only until the next
desired object comes along.

Things don't give us the security of being loved and
cared for. They weren't intended to. Those needs are
met in the framework of marriage harmony. Harmony is
a treasured commodity. Don't end up bartering over it.

▼ *Lord, help me to work with my spouse to create an
atmosphere of harmony in our home.*

HARMONY AT HOME—"FAMILY NIGHTS" HELP BUILD INTIMACY

Unless the LORD builds the house,
They labor in vain who build it.
—PS. 127:1

*M*any couples are like Jenice and Mark, who fought often over prioritizing family time with the kids. Jenice would complain; Mark would promise to do better. Jenice would get her hopes up, and then Mark would let her down because of other pressing priorities.

We encouraged Jenice and Mark to review their family time commitments and consider scheduling a family night each week. Such a night might include each family member committing to be on time for dinner together; children's homework completed; no friends over, no phone calls, and no interruptions; dinner conversation positive and appreciative (no rules, criticism, or conflicts); no TV while spending the next 1½ hours having fun. Take turns each week choosing a family fun activity.

For Jenice and Mark, family nights proved to be a hit with the kids and at the same time reduced a major conflict area. Jenice looked forward to making the night special with fun desserts for dinner and new game ideas. Mark enjoyed being able to protect his schedule for these family times and especially to find Jenice eager to see him and welcome him home.

▼ *Lord, build our home and our marriage according to Your blueprint.*

HONOR—TO TREAT AS "PRECIOUS" AND VALUABLE

> *Marriage is honorable among all.*
> —HEB. 13:4

$\mathcal{G}$od is a jealous God and He jealously guards His testimonies. He protected the Ark of the Covenant, bringing judgment upon those who would defile it. Remember the testimony of God's glory filling the Temple in 1 Kings 8, so awesome that none could stand. It was a testimony to Him and thus to be honored. Today the Ark is nowhere to be found and the Temple is in ruins, but a powerful testimony remains. Marriage is a testimony to Him and thus to be honored.

Teresa and I had been married several years before I began to "honor" our marriage with divine importance. Too many other priorities crowded it out. After God's gentle intervention in our lives, my priorities began to change.

 Lord, thanks for Your promptings concerning divine priorities.

HONORED BY THE GIFT OF GOD'S SON

You were not redeemed with corruptible things, like silver or gold . . . but with the precious blood of Christ —1 PET. 1:18

*O*ur Creator has "honored" us by the precious gift of His Son. His gift has declared our worth and value. Who am I that I should devalue what God has honored by the gift of His Son? To demean, neglect, or ridicule my spouse is to trample on the blood of Christ. Might this truth encourage my lips to speak only those things that edify.

Many couples find it startling when Teresa or I remind them that just because they *think* something, they *don't* have to *say* it! Hurtful words can't be taken back after they've wounded their "target." Remembering the great value that God has placed on your spouse makes it more difficult to say hurtful words.

 Thank You, Father, for prompting words that honor my spouse.

BE A READY LISTENER

A time to keep silence,
And a time to speak.
—ECCL. 3:7

I used to fear hearing David's thoughts and ideas. I'd fear because there were so many of them and I knew they'd affect my life in some way. David seems to have more ideas and plans than a person could get done in ten lifetimes! He'd be sharing some idea or dream with me and I'd be sitting there thinking up all the reasons why he couldn't or shouldn't do what he was just dreaming about.

One day he told me he felt as if he was in a skeet shoot. He'd throw out a thought and I'd be there to shoot it down. I want to hear David's dreams and ideas. I want him to continue to feel safe with me in his sharing and this can only happen when I honor him by being a good listener.

▼ *God, help me honor David by listening with my heart and not out of my fear.*

WIVES, HONOR YOUR "LITTLE BOY"

*An excellent wife is the crown of her husband,
But she who causes shames is like the rottenness in his bones.*
—PROV. 12:4

*T*om brought his wife, Andrea, for counseling so that we could "fix" her! He reported that she tried to be his "mother," always correcting him and competing with him over every decision. Andrea conceded this was often true, but she was trying to remind Tom that he wasn't perfect; she saw him as a "know it all" tough guy who had all the answers. Andrea was amazed to find underneath Tom's self-reliant exterior a somewhat insecure, frightened little boy, trying desperately to cover up his feelings of inadequacy.

Happy is the husband who has a wife and not a second "mother," a helpmate and not another boss, a "completer" and not a "competer." Every man seems to have a "little boy" inside of him who just wants to enjoy happiness with you, the girl of his dreams!

▼ *God, help me to encourage the little boy/little girl in my spouse.*

NOT SO GREAT EXPECTATIONS

In honor, giving preference to one another.
—ROM. 12:10

"I expect you to love me!" "I expect you to listen to me when I'm speaking."

Nasty word, *expect*. Have you ever stopped for a minute to examine what it implies?

When we say "I expect . . . ," we are basically saying we feel owed a specific kind of treatment and it had better be forthcoming.

Intimacy and expectations are mutually exclusive concepts. Assuming we get what we expect, we end up not really appreciating it. Or if they don't do what we expect, we get angry and try to make them pay.

Let me suggest an alternative—wants. Try to shift your next expectation into a want. "I want . . ." is a lot more hearable than "I expect . . ."

We dishonor our spouses when we expect things from them. We honor them by understanding they are free and by humbly presenting our needs to them. Honor your spouse—drop your expectations.

▼ *God, help me to honor my spouse by dropping my expectations and humbly presenting my needs.*

WHO'S ON FIRST?

The wise shall inherit glory.
—PROV. 3:35

Chris and I have had the pleasurable experience of building our home. It's been a special time drawing up house plans and then, step by step, watching the house become a reality in concrete, wood, pipes, and bricks. But we also have found that each of us likes to have the final say so. The decision to add this, take out that, choose colors was great fun as long as we agreed. But the times that we didn't there was friction.

Something like this will bring the selfishness out in you. And if things aren't settled quickly, your whole relationship can be contaminated. Sometimes I had to sit back, take a deep breath, and ask myself, What or who is more important, Chris or some house? Is what he is asking for so unreasonable?

Marriage is to be the place we treat our spouses with honor and as precious. We are to lift them up along with their needs and desires.

▼ *God, thank You for Your gift of my spouse. Help me to honor my spouse second only to You.*

HONOR YOUR PARTNER'S STRENGTHS

Let marriage be held in honor.
—HEB. 13:4 NASB

$\mathcal{O}$ ver the years, I've come to appreciate more and more Teresa's character qualities, the strengths within her that bless me and others. She is very supportive and loyal to me. She is convictingly diligent about getting her tasks completed. She is discerning and insightful, truthful and hospitable—just to name a few. Honoring your partner's character strengths is an important aspect of genuinely knowing him or her. Honoring your partner has its focus more on "who they are."

We ask couples to reflect on selected character qualities. Identify 3 to 5 that particularly exemplify your spouse. Is your spouse noted for contentment, creativity, forgiveness, or generosity? Do you appreciate his or her gratefulness, patience, resourcefulness, self-control?

After identifying positive character strengths, then share *private/verbal* praise—when the two of you are alone together: "I've been reminded lately of how much I appreciate you for your patience and sensitivity." A second challenge is to share *private/creative* praise. Send an appreciative note to the home or office; include a special note in a suitcase or lunch box, or stick one on a mirror or refrigerator! Finally, share *public praise*. In the presence of others, publicly appreciate your spouse for significant character qualities or accomplishments.

▼ *Help me look within and see the unique strengths You've blessed me with in my partner.*

HOSPITALITY—OPEN RECEPTION OF ANOTHER WITH A LOVING HEART

> *Be hospitable to one another without grumbling.*
> —1 PET. 4:9

*H*ospitality comes from a grateful heart. It's never from obligation, for that would lead to complaint. It's never from duty, for that would lead to pride. True hospitality comes from gratitude that the King of kings has swung open the gates of heaven to declare me a beloved saint and a joint-heir with Christ. He's attended to my every need by His grace. He initiates His daily loving-kindness without my even asking. It's this hospitality that I can now share with others.

We encourage couples to address each other more often with words of endearment—honey, sweetheart, dear. Such simple words, lovingly shared from a grateful heart, can bring a more inviting atmosphere to a relationship.

▼ *Thanks, Father, for the power of words that can warm hearts and encourage openness.*

JESUS, A GENTLEMAN

Behold I stand at the door and knock.
—REV. 3:20

*J*esus enters only into those places where He is welcomed. Only a stable welcomed His birth, so there He was born. Only sinners and the lowly welcomed His earthly ministry, so with them He cast His lot. Two discouraged Emmaus road disciples give a testimony of the hospitable heart: "Did not our heart burn within us while He . . . opened the Scriptures to us?" (Luke 24:32). Hospitality warms the heart as one is open to receive, to accept, to care, to give.

Early in our marriage, home was the last place either Teresa or I wanted to be. Teresa was stuck at home with kids all day. She remembers the fun of walking to the laundromat just to be around "big people." I often escaped into my own activities, fearful of marital conflict. Our healing journey into intimacy has made a difference. Home is a refuge; each of us longs to be there; it feels warm, inviting, secure.

▼ *Great Physician, thanks for healing our home.*

WELCOME HOME

If she has lodged strangers.
—1 TIM. 5:10

$\mathscr{D}$avid came home worn out at ten Wednesday night. Thursday morning he shared with me that he was just about to burn out. Going and giving too much was really about to take its toll. I knew he'd be home Thursday by seven and could let down some. I decided to make his evening one he would really enjoy.

I planned to grill fish, have baked potatoes, salad, and ice cream with blueberries for his meal. He loves to sit on our deck so we'd eat out there; then he could sit and enjoy being outside. Later I'd fire up the hot tub so he could totally relax before bed.

I wanted David to feel special. I wanted to share hospitality and go out of my way to make him feel welcome in our home.

▼ *I want my home to reflect hospitality, and I want the ones who live in it to feel it.*

"MAKE YOURSELF AT HOME"

Given to hospitality.
—ROM. 12:13

 $\mathcal{A}$ church in Ohio once arranged for me to stay in the home of a couple who were members. I don't like to do that because I feel I'm disrupting the normal flow of their lives. But the arrangements were set.

This couple could not have been more gracious. Whatever they could do for me, they did. They showed me true hospitality in action.

The message we are supposed to send to our spouses is, "Make yourself at home here in my life. You are welcome here. Whatever I have is yours." We are to let our spouses know that they are valued, joyfully invited into our thoughts and feelings, hopes and dreams.

Do you help your spouse feel at home in your life? Make your spouse comfortable inside your life; give them the best room in the house.

▼ *God, help me to open up my life to my spouse, sharing all I have, giving my best.*

COME ON IN—THE DOOR IS OPEN

Distributing to the need of saints, given to hospitality.
—ROM. 12:13

*J*odie was a minister's daughter. People watched her every move and remembered her every word. Whatever she felt on the inside, she hid it. The good of the family depended on it. So she become an actor on a stage playing a part, meeting the needs of those around her, not for God, but to create an impression. Pretty soon, the real Jodie—likes, dislikes, weaknesses, gifts—got lost in the shuffle. The one word she would have used to describe her life then was fear.

Then God brought Bob, her husband, into her life. Her fears began to melt away. Bob knows Jodie at her very core and accepts her. His loving and open reception gives her strength and confidence to risk.

▼ *Dear God, create in our marriage a place of security where we can be ourselves.*

A HOSPITABLE HOME—A CHILD WILL LEAD YOU

And a little child shall lead them.
—ISA. 11:6

*A*nn and Scott brought their three-year-old daughter Amy to their first appointment. Scott was frustrated over the lack of peace in his home, not feeling Ann's warmth and hospitality at the end of his long day. Ann complained of Scott's daily white-glove inspections of her housework. She had desperately tried to please him in her looks, cooking, and parenting, until she had finally given up and burst forth in rage, throwing things.

As we discussed Ann's periodic temper rages, Amy explored my office, touching everything she could reach, playing with the phone, and throwing pillows off the couch. After no more than five minutes into our session, Scott had told Amy at least twenty times: "No"; "Stop"; "Quit"; "Put that down"; "I'll spank you." Finally, in a fit of anger, Amy hit her dad with the phone. Both Ann and Amy had grown tired of performing for Dad's approval and were retaliating. Doing things for the approval, acceptance, and love of others reaps a hollow victory and robs a home of warmth and openness.

▼ *Help us share Your acceptance of us with each other and all who enter our home.*

SHOW HOSPITALITY TO "YOUR" SAINT

Be hospitable to one another.
—1 PET. 4:9

$\mathcal{D}$wayne and Julie had come to take each other for granted. Neither focused on any of the notable positive things about the other. They described a home atmosphere of distance and boredom now that their two children were away at college. After work on healing unresolved hurts, we spent time on restoring an "inviting," open relationship, taking the following steps.

First, begin keeping a *journal of gratefulness*. For one month, keep a written record of how God blesses you through your spouse. Enter the date, how you were blessed, and how you showed appreciation. This focus on blessings will help overcome a critical attitude, and showing appreciation will build up your spouse.

Second, begin to express *private praise*. Focus on character strengths. During a quiet, reflective time move toward your spouse—touch, give eye contact, verbalize your appreciation and love (start with cards if words are initially too difficult).

And finally, ask about *needs*—"I genuinely want to be the helpmate to you that God desires. As you identify ways I can be a better helpmate, please tell me." Dwayne and Julie took the challenge seriously and are now actively involved in helping other married couples.

▼ *Father, characterize our home by divine hospitality.*

INSTRUCTION—EQUIPPING FOR LIFE THROUGH WORDS AND EXAMPLE

Now the purpose of the commandment is love from a pure heart.   **—1 TIM. 1:5**

*E*ffective instruction must have a goal. Biblical instruction aims at a pure heart and expressed love. Biblical instruction has the Christ within His people as important examples. Paul reminds the Corinthians that they were living letters being "read" by others (2 Cor. 3:2). So it is with the Christian marriage and Christian family; those closest to us "read" us to learn of Christ.

Teresa and I had been married almost ten years with two children. I was reading and studying everything I could find on the Christian life. I tried every way imaginable to get my family as excited as I was. When I heard a conference speaker adapt a familiar saying to the Christian home—"Your wife and kids don't care how much you know until they know how much you care," I slowed down on trying to "know" everything and focused more on caring. It works!

▼ *Thanks, Father, for the power of caring.*

INSTRUCTION SAYS "FOLLOW ME"

*As You sent me into the world, I also have
sent them.*
                              —JOHN 17:18

 $\mathcal{P}$ aul was referred to me by his parents after several
times of sneaking out of his bedroom window at night to
join his friends for a night of mischief and pranks. Of
most concern to his parents was that Paul refused to
accept responsibility for his actions. "We want him to
see the wrong of his actions and apologize for the worry
and sleepless nights he's caused us," they insisted. Paul
wouldn't budge, only regretting that he had gotten
caught. In one family session, I asked Paul: "When is
the last time someone apologized in your family?" The
silence was telling; the parents squirmed on the couch.
Finally Paul responded: "Big people don't have to apologize, only kids. I've never heard Mom or Dad apologize to each other!" Example is the best teacher.

Couples most often know down deep that apology is
needed, but they wait for the spouse to apologize first.
Many have been waiting for years or even decades. True
love is willing to move first—even to apologize.

Christ did not say, "Do as I say, not as I do." His
instruction was first and foremost through His life, His
example. Christ came to live life and live it abundantly—so he could then give life and give it abundantly. So it is with true instruction: "Follow me" the
great teacher would say.

▼ *Keep me mindful, Father, of the example I set.*

BAD ATTITUDE

Let this mind be in you which was also in Christ Jesus.
—PHIL. 2:5

$\mathscr{I}$ only half-listen to David when he tries to instruct me in an area that I feel like I know more about than him. I turn him off mentally, interrupt him in the middle of his sentence to correct him, or if we're in the middle of a project that has its own instructions, I may pick them up to see if he's doing the project the way the instructions say. My attitude hurts David and drives a wedge between the two of us.

As I learn to allow David to help me and give up my know-it-all attitude, he asks more questions to see what I already know. When I trust his judgment, he is more likely to offer assistance. My attitude greatly affects our closeness.

 Lord, help me develop an attitude that willingly receives instruction.

INSTRUCTION FROM THE GREAT TEACHER

"Let the little children come to Me."
—MATT. 19:14

$\mathcal{G}$od accepts and loves us because we belong to His family. We don't have to *do* anything to win His love. Performance pressure creates an endless treadmill of doing things for the acceptance, approval, attention, and affection of others. People performing become "human-doings" rather than human beings.

Pressure is contagious. As I feel I must perform, then you begin to feel you must perform. Now the marriage begins to experience the bondage of conditional love.

The focus shifts from unselfish giving to selfish taking. Personal responsibility is replaced with justifying one's actions and blaming others. Self has been exalted, the Spirit grieved, and intimacy lost.

Leave the performance treadmill and enter into the joy of being a child of God. You'll be so grateful you won't be able to resist giving to each other!

 Thanks, Father, for the loving instruction from Your Son's example.

THAT WHICH HURTS INSTRUCTS

He who heeds the word wisely will find good.
—PROV. 16:20

$\mathcal{I}$t has been said that there are three rings in marriage: the engagement ring, the wedding ring, and the suffering. Many of us become disillusioned when we encounter the difficulties and problems inherent in marriage. When we hurt in our marriages, we may believe that something is horribly wrong.

Let me argue just the opposite. Marriage is inherently difficult, and facing those difficulties is painful. Yet the pain is trying to teach us about ourselves, specifically, to give up our selfish demands and expectations, to recognize our blind spots and weaknesses. Marital pain is a signal to work even harder.

The next time you feel unhappy in your marriage and start to think about quitting, don't. You are going through some necessary growing pains that signify the birth of a new, more mature you.

▼ *God, help me face my marital difficulties, accept pain as part of doing so, and trust You for growth.*

"I CAN'T BE OUT OF MONEY YET—MY CHECKBOOK STILL HAS CHECKS!"

Listen to counsel and receive instruction.
—PROV. 19:20

*F*inances are not my cup of tea! Fortunately, God blessed me with a husband who enjoys handling our finances. His filing system would make any CPA proud. As for me, I have trouble keeping my checkbook balanced.

Chris's meticulous record keeping has come in handy more times than I can count. Because of his work on our finances, we are in the best possible shape.

In recent years, he has taken more of an interest in showing me the financial ins and outs of our life. He cares enough about me and our family to teach me the things I need to know as his partner. I don't worry about the future as much because of that.

God wants us spouses to instruct each other lovingly in the things we have learned so that we can mature individually and as a couple. Our willingness to be instructed by each other is one way that we grow in wisdom.

▼ *God, help my spouse and me to be open to each other's instruction for the purpose of growing in wisdom together.*

INSTRUCTIVE ENCOUNTERS

*All Scripture is given by inspiration of God,
and is profitable for doctrine, for reproof, for
correction, for instruction in righteousness,
that the man of God may be complete,
thoroughly equipped for every good work.*
—2 TIM. 3:16–17

*A*my and Paul came to see us, frustrated by their lack of spiritual oneness. They only recently had made individual commitments to the Lord and become active in a local church. Neither came from a spiritual background, so they were hungry to make up for lost time. We began by encouraging them to read God's Word.

During a review of Scripture, Amy and Paul noted that we are given the opportunity to hear the Word from others (Rom. 10:17), read the Word (Rev. 1:3), study the Word (Acts 17:11), memorize the Word (Ps. 119:9), and meditate on the Word (Josh. 1:8).

In a follow-up session we talked about how many of these opportunities for encounter they were taking advantage of on a consistent basis. Each was challenged to review their weekly schedule, looking for places to insert other opportunities to encounter the Word—like a short time of meditation before bed or a specific weekly time allotted for intense, personal study of the Word. Amy and Paul grew together during these times in the Word. They later went on to seminary and will soon serve on the mission field.

▼ *Instruct us, Father, in Your word.*

INTIMACY—DEEP SHARING AND COMMUNION

And this is eternal life, that they may know You.
—JOHN 17:3

To be "born again" is to experience intimacy with our Creator. Ever since the Garden Fall, people have been born with a hunger for this intimacy. A God-shaped vacuum exists within the soul. No substitute will fill it. Only Christ will do. To "know" Him is to enter into eternal life; to receive Him is to allow Him to fill this emptiness and bring true intimacy. Then we can live in this intimate relationship as subsequent communion touches our souls. Awe and wonder accompany this communion and I am filled with joy inexpressible and full of glory" (1 Pet. 1:8).

Almost thirty years of marriage have confirmed to me an otherwise obvious truth. As I enjoy a daily intimacy with my Creator, my wife and kids benefit greatly.

▼ *Deepen my longing for intimacy with You, Father, my confidence that others will benefit.*

INTIMACY IS TO KNOW ME

O righteous Father! The world has not known You, but I have known You.
—JOHN 17:25

*H*e often declared that He only spoke those things He heard His Father speak. He only did those things He saw His Father do: "As I hear, I judge; and My judgment is righteous, because I do not seek My own will but the will of the Father who sent me" (John 5:30). Note the emphasis on *listening, discerning,* and then *responding.* Christ serves as our example and our instruction for intimate relationships.

Listening, discerning, then responding—these began to work with Teresa! To *listen* involved undivided attention, eye contact, and caring reflection. To *discern* involved looking past the words to find the feelings, the real impact of what Teresa shared. Then my *response* was from "her" world; she felt understood. So we experienced intimate moments together.

▼ *Thanks, Father, for the joy of "knowing" another and being "known" by her.*

SHEER OBEDIENCE

Let the husband render to his wife the affection due her, and likewise also the wife to her husband. —1 COR. 7:3

*D*avid and I married so young, we didn't have any concept of giving to meet each other's needs. We were trying to grow up and stay married at the same time. Years later I had become emotionally dead over the hurts that had occurred between us. David would ask me how I felt toward him and all I could say was, "I don't feel anything, I just feel dead on the inside." During this period, I knew I wasn't to withhold myself from David, that our sexual intimacy was to continue. As we worked through healing past hurts, I knew I was to continue giving to David even when the feelings weren't yet there.

Since we've learned how to heal our hurts, God has honored His promise to bring the feelings. Today I want sexual intimacy out of my desire to give and receive.

▼ *Thank You, God, for knowing what's best for us.*

INTIMACY OR INTERRUPTION?

Do not let your beauty be merely outward . . . rather let it be the hidden person of the heart. —1 PET. 3:3–4

Sherry and Mark sought counseling for Mark's "coldness." Sherry had heard we had "fixed" other husbands, and hers needed it badly! As I began to explore with Mark, he anxiously offered an opening sentence only to have Sherry interrupt. I again looked at Mark and asked him how it felt to be interrupted midsentence by his wife, only to have her interrupt again. Mark and Sherry had much work to do, but as hurts were identified and "blame games" stopped, Sherry became free to listen, and Mark "warmed up."

Intimacy is from the word *innermost* and relates to a vulnerable sharing of one's inner thoughts, feelings, and self. A man needs to feel secure in this sharing and confident of his wife's support through listening, empathy, and reassurance.

▼ *Father, free me to let down the protective walls that hide the real me.*

SUPER MARITAL BLISS?

*But if we walk in the light as He is in the
light, we have fellowship with one another.*
—1 JOHN 1:7

$\mathscr{I}$ have to laugh when I thumb through some of the
marital self-help books. To hear various authors tell it,
super marital bliss is available to anyone who wants it,
anytime, all the time.

To be honest, some days I feel lucky if I can pull off
being semidecent to Holly. Maybe I am setting my
sights too low, but more likely the bill of goods we are
sold is misleading.

Super marital bliss minute by minute in marriage is a
pipe dream. We will never be completely intimate with
our spouses. That possibility was lost when Adam and
Eve sinned in the garden.

Discouraging? It doesn't need to be. A deep, intimate relationship on a fairly consistent basis is a real
possibility.

The world's notion of super marital bliss is only going
to create chronic bitterness and frustration. But deep
intimacy is attainable with consistent effort and the
power of God working in your marriage.

▼ *God, help me to give up unrealistic notions about
marital intimacy, but to hold on to a belief in true
intimacy.*

THE TWO BECOME ONE

A man shall leave his father and mother . . .
and the two shall become one flesh.
—MATT. 19:5

$\mathcal{O}$ur marriage looks a lot different now than it did when we first started out. Time erodes idealism and exposes the futility of the world's shallowness. We saw up close what fallen sin nature looks like. Not only in our spouse but in ourselves as well.

Chris and I sought to draw closer to the Lord. Then He could begin His work of creating marital intimacy for our lives, the forging of two people, personalities, and goals into "one flesh."

Together we have seen the ugliness of sin and the beauty of victory in Christ. Together we have learned and are learning from past mistakes.

Though we have far to go, God has given us a love for each other by which we can hope all things, believe all things, and endure all things.

▼ *Lord, bind us together as a married couple. Help us to draw closer together and to be vulnerable.*

THE INTIMACY OF ROMANCE

When I found him whom my soul loves;
I held on to him and would not let him go.
—SONG 3:4 NASB

"*I* don't feel anything at all." "I just feel numb." Ken and Donna's romance was gone, mere existence having replaced it years ago. It was a rough counseling journey as old wounds were opened up and the painful healing process began. Serious childhood traumas needed attention, but Ken and Donna persevered, until little by little hope returned.

Keeping romance alive or rekindling it is essential for intimacy and abundance in marriage. At the appropriate time in our counseling we encourage couples to reflect and talk about romance—helping open up needed areas of vulnerability. Reminisce about their courtship—talk about their first date; early romance; silly, fun times together; favorite songs; dancing together; honeymoon fun! Ask about romance: "From your point of view how could we improve our marriage romance?"

Ken was encouraged to slip a love note in Donna's purse, shop for a personal gift; surprise her with flowers; plan a surprise picnic. Donna was encouraged to take the lead in verbalizing love, and giving compliments and expressing affection; initiating talk times and fun activities; and planning candlelight dinners at home alone. As Ken and Donna diligently put old things behind them and pressed on together, they enjoyed new intimacy.

▼ *Thank You, Father, for romantic love.*

KINDNESS—PLEASANT AND GRACIOUS SERVANTHOOD

Be kind to one another, tenderhearted.
—EPH. 4:3

*K*indness comes from a "tender" heart. It is betrayed by roughness and stoic indifference. Kindness is not genuine when strings are attached and never does it call attention to itself. True kindness springs from a heart softened by God's quiet love. Our Creator has "stooped" from heaven to serve us in the person of His Son; He has vulnerably revealed the loveliness of His heart in giving Christ in our stead.

We men have believed a lie; society has convinced us that to be "tender" is to be weak, less than a man. But tenderness of heart is our only hope for kindness. Many men have done the right things—they've bought flowers and remembered anniversaries—but without the tenderness of a caring and kind heart. The gifts then feel like obligations and duty. A wife needs to "feel" your care; begin to let your tenderness out.

▼ *O Father, open my heart that my spouse might see the depth of my feeling.*

KINDNESS AS ANOTHER'S PLEASANT SERVANT

> *As newborn babes, desire the pure milk of the word . . . if, indeed, you have tasted that the Lord is gracious.*
>
> —1 PET. 2:2-3

*K*indness begins with God at Calvary. No more gracious gift has been received. The tender warmth of this gift is the essence of kindness. Kindness is always connected to servanthood. Kindness, once tasted, produces a hunger for more. Sharing a taste of kindness encourages marriage closeness.

Kindness sees me as Teresa's pleasant servant! That didn't sound very appealing to this teenage husband. If I was pleasant, it wasn't from serving! And if I had to serve, I sure wasn't pleasant about it. Several years and much pain later, hope springs forth in faith as God's care touches and "tenderizes" my heart; caring for Teresa seems natural and not forced, a privilege and not duty.

▼ *O righteous Father, the world has not known You yet. Knowing You has made a lasting difference to me!*

LOVE MY BROTHER?

All of you be of one mind . . . , tenderhearted.
—1 PET. 3:8

$\mathscr{B}$eing kind to one another was a family priority when the kids were small. I wanted them to say thank you when someone shared their toys with them or when an adult served them. As the kids became teenagers, we seemed to grow out of making kindness a priority. Instead, issues like being home on time, getting homework done, and not wrecking the car became important. The habits we had developed of being kind to each other seemed suddenly foreign to the children during those teen years.

As the children have become adults, they have grown back into those habits we established early, though. Eric, our son, always says thank you after I've fixed his food or washed his clothes. Terri, Robin, and Eric all get along and are kind to each other without my standing over them. It's a joy to see kindness become a heritage we can pass on to our kids.

▼ *Train up a child in the way he should go.*

ABUNDANT KINDNESS

*Exceedingly abundantly above all that we
ask or think.*
                                    —EPH. 3:20

*J*oan and Allen had gone through the right motions
for twenty-plus years. They greeted each other with a
hug and verbalized their love; they regularly went on
dinner dates, and each did special little things for the
other. But now the nest was empty of their three children, and both were feeling empty and numb, committed to each other and to being kind, with little emotional
involvement.

Without adequate emotional skills or awareness,
adults often enter marriage hopeful of deep emotional
closeness but unable to achieve it. The friendship dimension of intimacy suffers as feelings of love, romance, and affection diminish. And the couples often
drift apart into separate worlds, a man absorbed in his
business or hobbies, a woman escaping into the world
of "super mom" or endless activity.

Joan and Allen had lost touch with their feelings in
fulfilling the daily duties of marriage and family. As they
learned to sense and experience their present feelings,
they were able to express empathy and comfort to each
other. Their kindness toward each other grew richer
with the added feelings.

▼ *Abundant thanks, Father, for feelings.*

HOW'D YOU KNOW THAT?

Love suffers long and is kind.
—1 COR. 13:4

$\mathcal{J}$ am a sports nut. There could be a nuclear war on page one of the newspaper, but what is important to me is who won what in sports the previous day.

Holly isn't a sports fan. She is more concerned about world hunger and homelessness. One day, though, she asked me, "Did you see where Roger Clemens threw a shutout yesterday?" I was sure Rod Serling was going to step out from behind a door and tell me I had just entered the twilight zone.

Her asking that question meant that she had come to make something important in her life just because it was important to me.

Kindness takes a lot of different forms. One is showing an interest in things that matter to your spouse. Showing an interest is another way to build an intimate marriage.

▼ *God, help me be kind, especially by taking an interest in things that matter to my spouse.*

IN MY HOUR OF NEED

Always pursue what is good both for yourselves and for all. —1 THESS. 5:15

I was lying in bed with a head cold, too sick to get anything done but not sick enough to go to the doctor. I had a million and one things to do—now I couldn't do any of them. Besides that, the kids still needed picking up from school, fed, bathed, and entertained. A thought ran through my mind: Am I too sick to run away from home, just for a day or two?

Then Chris called from work. "Holly, I know you've been feeling lousy, so I'll pick the kids up from school today and take them to the park. That way you'll have some time to rest. Don't worry about dinner. I'll bring some burgers home." He kindly canceled his plans to help me out at home. Emotionally I felt better already.

▼ *Father, help me to be sensitive to my spouse's needs and to respond with kindness in word and action.*

SMALL ACTS OF KINDNESS

Love is patient, love is kind.
—1 COR. 13:4 NASB

*T*eresa and I have enjoyed several very special times together—trips overseas, memorable gifts, a silver wedding anniversary—but the daily smaller things make just as much impact. It seems like it's the seemingly small things that often rob a marriage of intimacy; small acts of kindness that have stopped or become hindered in some way. We often encourage couples to talk together about these areas of kindness.

For us it's been important to take time for talking, relaxing together, dating your spouse, enjoying common interests, and weekends away. It's been significant to share feelings, fears, dreams, hopes, insecurities, and joys as well as your appreciation and gratefulness. We have found it imperative to give to your partner's need for affection, "foreplay" and sensitive "afterplay" as you focus on your partner's pleasure in sexual intimacy, considering his or her desires, preferences, and wishes. Finally for us it's been essential to initiate times of prayer, gentle touch, verbalized love, quiet closeness, and loving glances.

 Lord, keep me from rushing past the small expressions of kindness that can help keep love stirred up and warm.

LED—TO GO BEFORE ANOTHER AND SHOW THE WAY SO THE OTHER IS SECURE IN FOLLOWING

Lead me in Your truth and teach me,
For You are the God of my salvation.
—PSALM 25:5

*B*ob and I were talking about his openness to follow so he could better lead his family. "I'm still searching for someone to whom I can feel comfortable submitting," he said. "Then, I'll follow." That was almost twenty years ago, and Bob still hasn't found anyone he can submit to, and his family has suffered because of it. They've been plagued with church conflicts, rebellious kids, job stability, and tax problems. I'm not sure humbly submitting ever feels comfortable, but it is the key to good leadership.

God has taught me through some of the most unsuspecting people. A church custodian during my college years taught me much about the Bible; a loving grandfather showed a rebellious teenager much about acceptance, even when I didn't seem to want to learn. Struggling with my own hesitancies about following has helped me to be more sensitive when trying to lead.

▼ *What do You require of me, O God, but to love mercy, do justly, and walk humbly with my God?*

CHRIST NEEDED TO BE LED?

*And Jesus, being filled with the Holy Spirit,
returned from the Jordan and was led by the
Spirit.* —LUKE 4:1

*C*hrist being "led" . . . what a mystery! The perfect
God-man role models life in the Spirit, showing that he
does nothing of His own initiative (John 5:30). Rather,
He waits before the Father to be led. Only then can His
death be the sinless sacrifice for our sin. Only then do
we have the privilege to receive life in Him. How grateful I am that He yielded Himself to be led.

I struggle with not knowing what my wife needs! She
seems at times to be so different from me that my own
fear of inadequacy hinders me. It's helped me to acknowledge this struggle to God and to Teresa, and then
to be open to be led. I can then receive what God,
Teresa, and others have to offer.

▼ *Sharing the truth really does set you free!*

ARE YOU WILLING TO BE LED?

I find more bitter than death
The woman whose heart is snares and nets.
—ECCL. 7:26

$\mathscr{I}$ teach in my Basic Needs of a Man seminar that a man has a God-given need to be the leader in the home. In one session, an older woman asked what she should do when her husband wouldn't lead. I asked her, "Are you willing to be led?" Are you ready to tell him you will start letting him be a leader now?" Her answer was to turn her back on me and walk toward the door. I followed her and said, "Your turning your back on me answers my question." She again turned and left the room.

We desire to have our needs met, but sometimes we don't want to do our part. It's easier sometimes to say that when the other person changes, then I can do what I'm supposed to do.

Change in marriage can begin with only one person, but that person's heart has to be turned toward the Lord.

▼ *Father, I can only change when I keep my eyes on You.*

CHRIST'S EXAMPLE OF LEADERSHIP

Christ is the head of every man, and the man is the head of a woman.
—1 COR. 11:3 NASB

$\mathcal{V}$irginia and Ned were playing the classic power struggle game. Virginia was the most verbal and sought to control with words, threats, and explosions. Ned was rather quiet, inexpressive of feelings, and passive. He sought power by procrastinating, escaping into TV or work, and generally avoiding his wife. They genuinely loved each other, but it was hard to see.

Ned was shocked when I suggested that maybe Virginia's demands and explosions were her way of seeking a reaction from him—any reaction. Perhaps some of her reactions came from underlying fears about finances, disciplining the children, and the future. Virginia was looking for Ned's loving initiative and leadership in some of these areas. So together they developed a plan. Virginia and Ned agreed upon some parenting guidelines, and Ned began taking the lead in disciplining the kids when he was home. Ned contacted a financial planner, who worked with them on a family budget and retirement plan, and he began initiating couple dates, even finding the baby-sitter!

▼ *A husband can lovingly lead his wife through initiative, direction, and example.*

BY THE NOSE OR ARM IN ARM

Teach me Your way, O LORD
And lead me in a smooth path.
—PS. 27:11

*M*en like to joke about marriage. Some of the jokes are funny; some are cruel.

One thing I frequently hear men joke about, usually at each other's expense, is the "ring through the nose." When a man gets a good dose of this type of kidding, it threatens his ego. So the guy often tries to present the opposite image—"I run the show at my house, and the little woman does everything I tell her to do." John Wayne rides again.

These images are disturbing, and they miss the point of leading and being led. These images paint a picture of people trying to control and manipulate.

Marital intimacy involves a different type of leadership, an arm-in-arm style of facing problems together. Each person's view and feelings are equally important. If one takes the lead, it is a loving action meant to show the way so that the person following has a clear path.

▼ *God, help me to lead my spouse arm in arm, to help rather than to manipulate or control.*

WHERE YOU LEAD, I WILL FOLLOW

I have taught you in the way of wisdom:
I have led you in right paths.
—PROV. 4:11

*W*hy won't you let me lead?" The question asked in frustration and anger showed up off and on during our years of marriage. Chris and I would discuss our options; then after I had had my say I left the final choice to him. No sooner was the decision out of his mouth than I'd criticize him. Bottom line—I thought he'd made a bad choice. How would Chris ever learn to be an effective leader if he was not allowed to make choices and, yes, mistakes with no "I told you so's" to contend with.

God works through Chris to care for us. Trusting God to care for me means I must trust Chris to lead.

▼ *Dear God, help me not to arrogantly think I have all the answers. Give me a spirit of submission so that I might be led.*

LEADING YOUR MARRIAGE AFFECTIONATELY

*I am my beloved's
And his desire is for me.*
—SONG 7:10 NASB

*T*ouching always leads to sex," Lisa said angrily. Jay didn't have a clue as to the problem: "Why else would I want to touch?" he asked. He had no concept of the importance of non-sexual touching. Touch is one of the most powerful of our five senses, but too often couples deprive themselves of this pathway to closeness. For Jay and Lisa we recommended three "touch exercises" to increase closeness through non-sexual touching.

First, a *hand massage:* With palms up, begin tracing lightly your partner's palm; trace each finger all the way to the tip, touching each fingerprint in a light circular motion. Trace the inside of each finger, pausing to move back and forth where two fingers join at the palm. Second, a *foot bath:* take turns washing and bathing each other's feet. Don't talk, just relax; the purpose is not washing but relaxing and enjoyment. Use your hands or try a sponge also; be slow and don't rush. Finally, we suggested *synchronous breathing:* Lie facing each other and look into each other's eyes, close enough to feel your partner's breathing rhythm. Soon you will find a common rise and fall in your inhalation/exhalation. Alter this pattern by fitting like spoons—her back against his abdomen. After breathing is synchronized, close your eyes and just relax, feeling the sensations.

▼ *Lead us, Father, into the intimacy You desire.*

LOVE—COMMITTED TO "DOING GOOD"

Love one another; as I have loved you.
—JOHN 13:34

$\mathcal{T}$he Father's firm commitment to love us allows me to then love. His commitment was made toward me in spite of God knowing all about me. My present failures are no surprise to Him. I've often contemplated how different marriage would be if lived from this same vantage point of divine love.

The next time Teresa fails me in some way, might God remind me that it's already been taken into account and that my love remains firmly committed to her. True love is an unconditional commitment to an imperfect person. The perfect person and perfect conditions won't ever be found. Can you receive, then share, God's love anyway? Such is the only hope for an intimate marriage.

 Thanks, Father, for Your unconditional commitment to me, an imperfect person.

RETURN TO YOUR FIRST LOVE

Keep yourselves in the love of God, looking for the mercy of our Lord Jesus Christ unto eternal life.
—JUDE 21

If I don't feel close to God, guess who moved? He's still right where I left Him! God's love is a firm commitment, but I choose whether to abide in its abundance or walk after the deeds of the flesh: immorality, strife, jealousy, outbursts of anger, disputes, drunkenness, carousing (Gal. 5:19–20). These sound an awful lot like the presenting problems in marriage counseling! When loving my spouse seems a struggle, it's time to return again to my first love.

What things about your spouse originally attracted you to him/her? What little ways did you express care and love for one another? What enjoyable ways did you spend time together? Returning to these ingredients of "first love" helps many couples renew perspective, gain hope and move beyond past hurts as they are healed.

▼ *Stir us often, Lord, with remembrances of our first love.*

I LOVE YOU FIRST

We love Him because He first loved us.
—1 JOHN 4:19

*D*avid said one day that he'd be glad when I said, "I love you" first. David was wanting me to initiate statements of love. It wasn't that I didn't love him or that I was afraid to share my feelings with him; I just didn't think about it. I wasn't taught to share my feelings aloud. After I left home, Mother would sign her letters with "I love you," but I never heard her say the words.

I can look back and see the change that took place in my life when I received Christ's love first. When I saw how Christ loved me, I could love myself. How could I have possibly given what I didn't feel?

David also gave and kept giving me his love. He's never loved me conditionally but rather with the unconditional love of Christ. Having received love from God and David, I'm finding it easier to share my love.

▼ *Thank You, Father, for Your unconditional love.*

"HIDERS" STRUGGLE TO FEEL LOVE

A time to keep silence
And a time to speak.
—ECCL. 3:7

*N*othing's wrong." "It really doesn't matter." These are classic lines from a person who hides feelings of hurt, irritations, and unmet needs while inside pain or anger seethes. Rather than "cause problems" or risk rejection, the hider seeks to suffer in silence.

By hiding our own feelings and desires, we undermine our own self-worth and sow the seeds in inevitable retaliation.

Often those who've hidden their true feelings for years complain that they can't feel love. Resentments have quenched romance. Bitterness has squelched affection.

A caring, loving relationship is built on the secure knowledge that if I'm feeling lonely, hurt, or disappointed, my spouse will want to know!

▼ *I'm grateful, Father, that Teresa wants to know of my need and my hurt.*

BUMPER STICKERS AND LOVE

What a man desires is unfailing love.
—PROV. 19:22

I love bumper stickers. One that I saw a few months ago said, "Of all the things I've lost, I miss my mind the most." I can identify.

One bumper sticker says, "I love my wife" or "I love my husband."

It is rather sad that loving one's spouse has seemingly become such a rare thing that some feel compelled to proclaim it on the rear end of their cars, almost as if to say, "Hey, I know you hate your spouse, but I love mine!"

Wouldn't it be something to live in a world where loving one's spouse was so common that no one would even think of putting a bumper sticker on their car to proclaim it?

 God, help me to love my spouse deeply, proclaiming that love through my actions each day.

LOVE IS FOREVER

*Husbands, love your wives, just as Christ also
love the church.*   —EPH. 5:25

J watched him look into the window and check his reflection. He carefully combed his hair and straightened his tie. He had to be seventy years old, yet he acted as eager as a schoolboy. He was a regular visitor to the local nursing home. He was meeting his wife, a victim of Alzheimers. His wife never spoke much. But it didn't seem to matter to him that he got no response from his wife. He made cheery conversation, read letters from family, sang to her, fed her, or just held her hand.

Love, a *rare* commitment to care for another regardless of how the response. Christ took human form to give us that love—at the cross. Mr. Lacy is pitied but a privileged man, who loves his wife in such a way that the world may look on with a deep sense of longing. He paints a beautiful picture for the rest of us to see and enjoy what Christ's love for us looks like.

▼ *Lord, thank You for giving Your only Son. Teach me
to love my spouse by Your definition.*

LOVING YOUR SPOUSE SPIRIT, SOUL AND BODY

They shall become one flesh.
—GEN. 2:24

*T*hree different Greek words for love reinforce for us the dimensions of marital intimacy. We discuss each word with couples, reflecting on needed personal improvement. The word *Agape* is used in the New Testament to describe the attitude of God toward His Son (John 17:26), toward humanity (John 3:16), and toward those who believe in His Son (John 14:21). *Agape* is then used to convey God's desire that believers share this love with others (John 13:34). *Agape* is shown through its action, commitment, and giving—not through its feeling. *Agape* is an expression of God's Spirit and is impossible to produce through self-will.

The word *phileo* is distinguished from *agape* in that it speaks of tender affection and represents the emotional aspect of a relationship. This feeling aspect of love is quenched when hurts are unresolved. *Phileo* speaks of two hearts knit together in tenderness of mutual companionship. A descriptive characterization would be to affectionately cherish a special person. Finally, *eros* is the word from which *erotic* comes; it speaks of sensual fulfillment and the physical pleasures of sexual expression. A God-given boundary to confine these pleasures to the marriage relationship is given often in the Scriptures (see Heb. 13:4).

▼ *Heavenly Father, help us enjoy our love for each other so we can testify of Your plan for marriage.*

MERCY—A CARING MINISTRY OF HELP TO ONE IN NEED OR DISTRESS

You have heard of the perseverance of Job and . . . that the Lord is very compassionate and merciful.
                    —JAMES 5:11

*M*ercy touches us at the point of pain; mercy ministers at a time of loss. Life inevitably brings both; but a deeper tragedy is enduring them alone! During life's pain and loss every part of my being cries out "does anyone care?" Mercy answers, "I care and I'm here with you." Mercy is most often the comforting support of one's presence. It's the reassuring touch of mercy that draws me away from future anxiety into the security of present love.

Couples often benefit from sharing "pain points" with each other. As I reflect on such times of pain and loneliness, the sensitive comfort and caring touch of a merciful spouse cries out within me, *I'm no longer alone!*

▼ *Thanks, Father, for the blessing that comes from being comforted in mourning.*

GOD IS NOT BANKRUPT!

*God, who is rich in mercy, because of His
great love with which He loved us.*
—EPH. 2:4

*T*here will be no mercy "shortage." God is rich in it.
All too often marriage brings together two emotionally
bankrupt partners who go into the marriage "business." Neither has much to give the other, and they both
begin a "taking" cycle that brings anger and disappointment.

Codependency is a common descriptive expression
today of such a "taking system," two people overwhelmed with their own neediness, each trying desperately to take from the other.

The only real solution is access to God's unlimited
supply. Welcome to the kingdom where God is the God
of *all* comfort; where God *is* love; and where God is *rich*
in mercy.

▼ *Thanks, Father, for the completeness of Your
promises.*

GIVING OUT OF GOD'S RESOURCES

Through the mercy shown to you, they also
may obtain mercy.   —ROM. 11:31

$\mathcal{D}$avid and I are so grateful to God for showing us mercy throughout the first ten years of our marriage. Our marriage was not made in heaven. When we received Christ as our Savior, God started to heal our marriage and to use our past to help mend other hurting marriages. Since we've experienced God's mercy in our marriage, it's easy to give other couples mercy.

One special gift of mercy we can give is to minister to missionaries and other couples working to serve God. It's very hard to find someone to share your problems with when you're in church-related work. Everyone expects you to hear problems, but not have them. David and I can show mercy by being available to hear their personal problems without their feeling judged.

▼ *Father, because of Your mercy, we can show mercy.*

MERCY FLOWS FROM A TENDER HEART

One who by the mercy of the Lord is trustworthy. —1 COR. 7:25 NASB

*M*y husband has as much feeling as a machine." "She makes love to me with as much passion as a cardboard box." These are common complaints from married people in our high-tech society. Couples want to "feel" love but have no idea of what feelings are!

Our world seems to emphasize achievement and performance to the exclusion of emotional development. Young children learn to tie shoes and count to ten, but who helps them identify their feelings? Older children begin the treadmill of endless activities—Scouts, dance, sports, piano—but how do they learn to deal with normal rejections, fears, and disappointments? Adolescents focus on athletics, academics, or popularity, but how do they heal hurts from normal tension? Most don't get them healed but get married instead!

Our work with couples has to start with the emotional basics. Feelings are *not* opinions. "I feel like you're not handling the kids right" is an opinion. "I feel lonely when we've not had quality private time together" is a feeling. We help couples learn to name feelings as they experience them and work on healing unresolved feelings from the past as anger is put away (Eph. 4:31), fear is cast out (1 John 4:18–19), and mourning is comforted (Matt. 6:5). From a tender heart, couples can enter into the joy of marriage as God intended.

▼ *Thanks, Father, that You've made me able to feel.*

HAVE MERCY ON ME, PLEASE!

What does the LORD require of you?
But to do justly,
To love mercy.
　　　　　　　　　　—MIC. 6:8

*W*e all mess up. One of our biggest fears is that the person on the receiving end of the mistake will make us pay big time.

When, instead, our mistake is met with mercy, it is a wonderful experience. Instead of blasting us, the person tries to help us. Whew!

We make a lot of mistakes in marriage, that's for sure, and we sometimes desperately need our spouses to show mercy. When they do, there is healing power. When they don't, the pain worsens.

Marriage requires a merciful attitude. With it, we become what God intended us to be—mature, deeply loving people.

Shown any mercy to your spouse lately?

▼ *God, help me to show care and concern to my spouse, to be especially merciful when I have been wronged.*

THANKS! I NEEDED THAT

Mercy triumphs over judgment.
—JAMES 2:13

Sue finished the final page of her research paper. She'd been writing in longhand for a week. She would graduate in the spring after all. She was afraid her procrastination had cost her meeting the deadline, but she had two more days to type, correct, and print out the paper. And Barry would show her how to do that on their new computer as soon as he got back from his business trip. She could see herself now, in her cap and gown walking across the stage . . . when the phone rang. It was Barry. His trip had been extended to all of next week. No cap, no gown, no graduation! "I'll tell you what," Barry continued. "I'll call back tonight after my last meeting and take you through step by step using the computer. And I won't get off until you've got it, okay?"

Sue didn't deserve his kindness, but she badly needed it. Her husband cared enough to sacrifice his own time for her. She'd graduate after all.

▼ *Lord, help me to show mercy in my marriage, to give what my spouse needs.*

HOW DO YOU FEEL?

*Should you not also have had mercy on your
[brother] even as I had mercy on you?*
—MATT. 18:33 NASB

*E*ach of us experiences emotion. Some share their
feelings openly while others hide them. Some seem
overly sensitive to emotion, while others are unsure of
what they feel. The same emotion can be expressed in
greatly differing ways. Loneliness in some might be expressed by sad withdrawal, while others might express it
through endless conversation. A major ingredient in relational closeness is the open and constructive expression of emotion. A first step is to develop an emotional
vocabulary. To encourage emotional sharing in your
marriage, take turns naming as many emotions as you
can.

Very often a person might identify anger as a felt
emotion, but in reality this anger might be the sum of
feeling unappreciated, rejected, and misunderstood.
Why is it important to identify emotions? One reason is
that many emotions define for us major emotional
needs we have, feeling unappreciated means we need
appreciation; feeling rejected implies needing acceptance; and feeling misunderstood implies the need for
understanding. Take turns sharing recent emotional
needs you have identified.

▼ *Father, let Your mercy through me care that my
spouse often feels pain.*

PEACE—HARMONY BASED ON VALUING ANOTHER

And His name will be called
Wonderful, Counselor, Mighty God,
Everlasting Father, Prince of Peace
—ISA. 9:6

The deceitfulness of riches and the cares of this life choke out true marital joy. Career "ladder climbing," the super-mom syndrome, and extra-marital affairs all cause their tragic share of marital misery by stifling intimacy and creating fear from betrayal. Possessions can't buy happiness, and social status can't bring inner joy.

Into this pain-filled world, in the city of David, a child was born. He was—and is the Prince of Peace!

▼ *Thanks, Father, for sending the Prince of Peace.*

PEACE IN SPITE OF DIFFERENCES

Be at peace among yourselves.
—1 THESS. 5:13

*P*eace is an inner tranquility of relatedness that springs forth from a common source. Differences between us and others tend to produce anxiety and not peace. Great differences can produce considerable anxiety. But we can experience a peace that the world doesn't know. This peace comes from the commonality of faith in the One who holds the world, who knows our common human condition, divine deliverance, and eternal hope.

Anxiety or tension over "differences" pushes many couples apart. Teresa and I differ over punctuality, bedtime, exercise, money, and disciplining kids. Underneath all these differences, we each share a need for love, attention, and comfort. Peace comes in sensing that the other knows and cares!

▼ *Thanks, Father, for the commonality of need.*

PEACE WITHIN OUR BORDERS

May peace be within your walls.
—PS. 122:7

$\mathcal{O}$ne side of our corner lot is completely natural with lots of trees that come up to our deck. The landscaping on the side of our home next to the street is unfinished, so it's not the best view from our deck. David was enjoying being outside one evening when I came out to join him. He'd completely relaxed after work and was at total peace. I'd been out only a few minutes when I totally ruined his peace by my attitude.

I have a tendency to be a half empty person. When I came outside, I could see only everything wrong with our back yard. I started complaining over what we hadn't accomplished instead of enjoying what we did have. David challenges me to see life in a more positive way. As I do, I find more peace.

▼ *Peace is a reward for a positive attitude.*

SHARING THE TRUTH IN LOVE
PROMOTES TRUE PEACE

Speaking the truth in love.
—EPH. 4:15

*H*oney, I'm sure you didn't mean to, and yet it hurt when you seemed to side with the kids over me when I asked them to get in bed." Doesn't this seem to be a better way to handle conflict rather than "I'm sick of you always siding with the kids." Couples can learn to "speak the truth in love."

Hurts, irritations, and unmet needs are inevitable in close relationships. In fact, closeness actually magnifies daily irritations. In the family, admittedly imperfect people are thrust together into close proximity. The family stress is further intensified by the tendency to drop the public "mask" of being nice at home.

An expectation of intimacy without conflict is unrealistic. Learning to resolve conflict by speaking the truth in love will actually deepen intimacy and encourage peace.

▼ *Lord, remind me to speak truth in love.*

A PLACE OF PEACE

Let the peace of God rule in your hearts.
—COL. 3:15

$\mathcal{I}$ have been blessed with the opportunity to do personal growth seminars across the country. I greatly enjoy doing them, and the people in each of the places I have gone are always so gracious.

Yet I always feel somewhat anxious when I travel. It isn't related to thinking something bad might happen to me or Holly and the kids while I'm gone. It is anxiety born of being away from home, my place of peace, where I feel anchored. No matter how unpredictable life may be, home feels stable and good.

Dorothy in *The Wizard of Oz* was right. There is no place like home. I miss it when I am away. It is great to return home after a seminar and know Holly and the kids will be there with smiles on their faces and love in their hearts when I pull into the driveway.

 God, thank You for marriage, family, and my home. Please help them to be a continual place of peace.

ONE FOR ALL AND ALL FOR ONE

The fruit of righteousness is sown in peace by those who make peace. —JAMES 3:18

*K*en dearly wanted to go to seminary. It had been his life's dream. Kay, his wife, wanted to help him. So together they planned for Kay to get a full-time job outside the home. The kids would have to be in day care for half-days.

About halfway through the year Ken saw his wife begin to change. Kay lost her temper more often, blowing up at the littlest things. She looked pale and downcast. He knew she had a very difficult boss and that she hated that the kids were in day care. The situation was tearing her apart. Ken's wife came first. If God wanted him to continue seminary, He would have to provide funds for them in another way. Kay needed to quit.

Marriage is at the top of our list, even over other important good things.

▼ *Lord, give me such a longing for peace that I will meet the needs of my spouse over my own.*

A PEACEFUL HOME

An excellent wife, who can find?
She opens her mouth in wisdom,
And the teaching of kindness is
*   on her tongue.*
—PROV. 31:10, 26 NASB

$\mathcal{A}$ wife has a special role in contributing to the emotional atmosphere of the home. Teresa often encourages a wife to bring up the subject: "In wanting to be the wife of a genuinely happy husband, I'd appreciate your sharing with me little ways I could make you happy." She might also encourage wives to study husband happiness by reviewing Proverbs 31 and 1 Peter 3:1–7.

To help establish a more peaceful home environment, we encourage couples to cheerlead each other. Send each other off each day with encouragement, gratefulness, and affectionate caring. Welcome each other home with empathy, understanding, and tenderness. Publicly and privately offer praise. Pamper each other. Surprise each other with a favorite meal, breakfast in bed, a surprise date, or a passionate evening alone.

Each partner must bridle the tongue. Turn negative comments or criticism into words that edify (Eph. 4:29). Notice the difference: "You care more about your career than you do me!" versus "I know you've been very busy with work, and I feel both appreciative of your diligence and lonely to be with you. I'm looking forward to spending some time alone together soon."

▼ *Father, give our marriage Your peace, which the world does not know.*

PRAISE—COMMENDING MEANINGFUL CONTRIBUTION

Who is like You, O Lord, among the gods?
Who is like You, glorious in holiness,
Fearful in praises.   **—EX. 15:11**

*T*he psalmist's rhetorical question is quite fitting: *None* is like You, O God! Praise has no real definition apart from the wonder of our Creator. He gives the word its meaning and in so doing defines our purpose.

A negative, critical environment is not conducive to intimacy. Many we see characterize their partners as complainers, nags, or worse. We often encourage individual attention to each partner's devotional life of praise.

You can't leave the presence of Jehovah with a critical tongue or downcast look. Praise in the presence of your Lord will put honey on your lips and joy in your face. Many a home could benefit from a revival of praise.

▼ *None is like You, O God; praise the Lord.*

A WIN-WIN EXPERIENCE

A man is valued by what others say of him.
—PROV. 27:21

$\mathcal{P}$raise is genuinely a win-win proposition. The "recipient" of praise feels great having been acknowledged as significant and important. The "giver" of praise is blessed with a grateful heart and guarded from a critical spirit.

We often use praise-sharing in our couples, group work. Couples tell each other things like, "I feel especially loved by you when ＿＿＿＿＿." They each share their responses with the group. This helps give each partner a better understanding of how their partner best "feels" love. Then each couple faces one another, holds hands, and verbalizes their response to their partner. The partner "receives" the expression of appreciation and acknowledges it positively in some way. Each can begin to experience the win-win of praise.

▼ *Thanks, Father, for the privilege and power of praise.*

GIVE HIM A BREAK

If there is any virtue and if there is anything praiseworthy—meditate on these things.
—PHIL. 4:8

$\mathcal{D}$avid and I seemed to be going in two different directions with our finances. I wanted to save more, and I felt David was trying to spend more. One weekend I had been in South Carolina doing a conference and David had been in Tennessee doing school work. We met in Atlanta on Saturday evening to spend the night.

David had made reservations for us at a resort and checked out Underground Atlanta. Instead of praising him, my first thought was how much extra money we would be spending. God impressed me to praise David for his efforts and his thoughtfulness instead of being so negative. I could have ruined our fun if I'd been critical instead of giving David praise.

▼ *Lord, thank You for helping me change my thoughts.*

THE POWER OF PRAISE

Let another man praise you, and not your own mouth.
—PROV. 27:2

*C*ouples we visit with have often overlooked the power of praise. Wives particularly seem to underestimate the power of their words. Men can often appear so aloof or self-assured that you would never think they needed a wife's praise.

I remember Lewis's constant criticism of his wife, Andrea, for how she spent money. Lewis and his wife obviously didn't lack for money. Was Lewis just "tight" and critical by nature? Andrea began to express appreciation and praise for her husband's diligence and wisdom, publicly praising him for his faithful provision to the family. This is what Lewis really needed, his wife's praise. His criticism stopped.

Through her words, a helpmate has a particular ministry in building up her spouse.

▼ *Guard my lips, Father, that my words might only exalt and edify.*

FAINT PRAISE

Her children rise up and call her blessed;
Her husband also, and he praises her.
—PROV. 31:28

*I*sn't it a great feeling to be praised for something you've done? There is hardly anything like it.

Sadly, most marriages are pretty praise deficient. Praise, when it is offered, is often "faint" at best. Kind of like, "That dress doesn't look all that bad."

We need praise to keep going in life. Like children, we need someone to notice our effort and talents and "stroke" them. The praise needs to be clear, strong, and accurate.

Praise your spouse about the things that really are good about him/her. Don't let your praise be faint. Make it loud and clear.

▼ *God, help me offer praise to my spouse regularly, clearly, and honestly.*

WORDS OF REFRESHMENT

A wholesome tongue is a tree of life,
But perverseness in it breaks the spirit.
—PROV. 15:4

*A*nn's parents had an awful marriage; her father was a weak man and her mother was too controlling. So Ann felt it her special task to keep her own marriage from suffering the same fate. Her helpful comments on her husband's behavior slowly deteriorated into stinging criticisms. He became weak and withdrawn. Because Ann and her husband had a real commitment to their marriage, they decided to seek counseling. Ann learned her husband had experienced criticism as a child and was dealing with it as he had then. For protection he withdrew into his own world.

One helpful thing was for Ann to give her husband one praise a day. Through perseverance she began managing more than one. Her husband began responding with more openness, sharing his day and his struggles. She started listening more. Soon things started improving.

▼ *Father, help me to delight in giving words of praise to my spouse.*

GOD DID GOOD!

He did good . . . filling our hearts with food and gladness.
—ACTS 14:17

$\mathcal{G}$od did good! What an understatement. He did good because that's His nature. He's not a celestial killjoy but a caring Father who desires not to withhold any good thing from us. His longing is that we might come to enjoy everything pertaining to life and godliness. Enjoying another person is a special part of God's plan for marriage as two people come to find a special joy in each other's company. God did good when He created your partner—just for you!

It's amazing how many couples come to counseling with a mind-set that, at best, marriage is to be tolerated. Coping is the most they hope for; surely, they think, they've done great if they just somehow stay married. Into this attitude of mediocrity and complacency comes a God who desires to give life and give it abundantly. This doesn't mean special protection from problems, but it does mean joy, peace, and liberty in the midst of them. Part of His plan for such abundance are the divine relationships through which He's chosen to work: marriage, the family, and the church.

▼ *Thanks, Heavenly Father, for being a good God!*

PRAYER—ENTREATING GOD
TO FAVOR ANOTHER

Give ear to my prayer, O God.
—PS. 55:1

$\mathcal{G}$od's provision for communion through prayer speaks much of His character. He sought us and thus established this divine channel. He listens for our cry as a mother listens for her young. He knows my voice and attends to my cry. Such is my God: a God of loving initiative, who seeks me; a God of great sensitivity, who listens for me; a God of intimacy, who knows me; and God of grace, who attends to my needs.

It's important to entreat God's attention and favor for your spouse. Prayers of thanksgiving can be an important opportunity for closeness. Requesting prayer as you leave in the morning gives opportunity to be likeminded during the day. Prayer helps draw couples together.

 Thanks, Lord, for the special privilege of sharing together in prayer.

PRAYER HELPS HEAL HURTS

Pray for one another, that you may be healed.
—JAMES 5:16

There may be no more powerful healing tool for relationships than prayer. Amid every argument in marriage, couples can find common ground in yielding prayer: "Not my will but Your will be done." There's an important healing message as two agree in prayer, declaring their dependence upon their Creator. When couples declare together God's greatness their pride is shattered, their relationship healed.

We often encourage couples to pray together after a time of confession and forgiveness. Since marital hurts are inevitable, confession and forgiveness need to become a regular practice. First, they apologize: "I see that I've hurt you by my impatience and sharp words. Will you forgive me?" Then, they can forgive (remembering that God has already forgiven them). Afterward, they can pray. Physical intimacy is often the result.

▼ *Thanks, Lord, for Your healing plan.*

SOMEONE WITH SKIN ON

Prayer for you.
—2 COR. 9:14

$\mathcal{I}$ know I can pray for myself and God hears me. There are times when I know He wants me to rely on Him alone. I also know God has given me someone with skin on to pray with me. In an especially hard day, I want David to pray for me. I always feel a lot closer to him when we've prayed.

I also seem to be able to cope with my situation better when I've had an opportunity to share with David and then he led us in prayer. David's being the leader and authority in our home weakens the evil one and his attack upon us when we've joined together in prayer. When I've received the prayers of David and we've agreed in prayer on the problems, I feel I can walk through my trials with the attitude of an overcomer.

 Father, thank You for giving me someone with skin on to pray in my behalf.

LOOKING UNTO HIM

My God shall supply all your needs.
—PHIL. 4:19

$\mathcal{A}$ndy and Patti came for counseling during their first year of marriage. Love had already died; resentments had quenched romance. Common but painful dynamics were identified in our first session. "Patti expects dinner out twice a week and a $300/month clothes budget, so I give it to her whether we can afford it or not." "Andy expects sex twice a week and my companionship at company functions, so I accommodate him whether I feel like it or not." Andy and Patti's expectations of each other were "killing them."

Where do I direct my expectations for meeting valid human needs? God often involves others in ministering to human need. Expecting God to meet needs in accordance with His Word will prompt a faith that He can work through others.

Andy and Patti began to "faith" their own needs to God and give to each other.

▼ *Thanks, Father, for Your provision that frees me to give.*

THE COUPLE THAT PRAYS TOGETHER, STAYS TOGETHER

Is anyone among you suffering? Let him pray.
—JAMES 5:13

$\mathcal{I}$ was having lunch with a friend of mine one day, and we got to talking about what makes a marriage a good one. He mentioned he had been doing a lot of thinking about that. He shared with me that after reading all kinds of books and talking with all kinds of people, he had decided that the most important element in making a marriage healthy and successful is prayer.

That lunch conversation stuck with me. At the time, I was not praying with Holly on a regular basis. My friend's conclusion seemed pretty much on target, and I talked to Holly about it.

We decided that regular prayer was lacking in our marriage. We began to pray more often together, and what a difference it made. Prayer humbles you before each other, and it makes you more accountable.

▼ *God, help us to take prayer seriously in our marriage.*

YOU'RE NOT IN THIS ALONE

Is anyone among you suffering? Let him pray.
—JAMES 5:13

$\mathcal{I}$ am a worrier, and I come from a long line of worriers. When I was asked to help write this devotional, I was very excited. The closer to the deadline I got, the more anxious and apprehensive I became. What will the quality of my work be? Will I finish on time? What if David, Teresa, and Chris secretly wish they'd never asked me to help? So there I was, standing in the middle of the room, stressed out, not sure what to do next when Chris popped his head out of the bedroom door. "I've noticed how anxious you have been, so I prayed God would grant you a peaceful and calm spirit." Wow, talk about a shot in the arm! Chris noticed my behavior, listened as I shared my concerns, and cared about my problems. He could have gotten upset with things that I had let slide, like housework, but he prayed instead. Chris's belief encouraged me.

▼ *Father, help me to remember to lift up my spouse's needs to You in prayer.*

BEGINNING SILENTLY

*If two of you agree on earth about anything
that they may ask, it shall be done for them
by My Father who is in heaven.*
—MATT. 18:19 NASB

*M*any of the couples we counsel come to desire a closer spiritual relationship. We're often asked where to start in this journey. Begin with occasional silent prayer together. One recent survey indicated fewer than 15 percent of churchgoing couples pray together. The reasons are obvious. "I'm not exactly sure what to say." "I would not pray as good as the minister," or "I might get corrected by my spouse!"

We might give this one simple recommendation: Spend a few minutes talking about things that matter—concerns, hopes, dreams, or fears; kids or work or money or feelings or future events. This might come at the close of a marriage staff meeting or during the last minutes before sleep; just grow together in it.

Then simply reach over and take each other by the hand (a husband's initiative here as "leader" seems appropriate). Pray together silently for a short 2 or 3 minutes. If you become comfortable praying out loud, fine, and if not, fine. Most of the time couples sense an important spiritual closeness and many report that physical closeness often follows.

▼ *Father, there's possibly nothing more powerful than two people in prayerful agreement. Let it be so for us.*

PROTECTION—STANDING BETWEEN MY MATE AND HARM

So will the LORD of hosts defend . . . deliver
. . . preserve.   —ISA. 31:5

*I*t's good to have the Lord of Hosts as your protector. Others might be helpful, supportive, and encouraging, but with Jehovah you will prevail. Nothing escapes His notice, and no obstacle stands in His way. The sheltering wing of His protection provides safety and security. When I need someone standing between me and the adversary, I'm glad it's God. When I fear, His perfect love awaits to cast out all fear. When life's daily provision seems lacking and pressures abound, His testimony cries out of His provision: Consider the lilies of the field and the birds of the air. Be not anxious. Your protector is here.

Marriage intimacy relates somehow to this growing sense of security, knowing that there's also a person with flesh and blood that I can lean upon to "be there" for me.

▼ *Protect, deliver, rescue . . . we need You, Father.*

PROTECTED BY WISDOM FROM ABOVE

Wisdom strengthens the wise.
—ECCL. 7:15

The psalmist spoke of my tendency to wander like the sheep, but God's wisdom protects me as I choose my steps. God's wisdom protects me from straying as discernment is given for daily life. God sees it all, the big picture. He sees the end from the beginning and the last step before the first is taken. Such wisdom will obviously protect me. Such wisdom will also give me something to share as I seek to love this special spouse God has given me.

As we encourage couples in their spiritual growth together—studying devotions, memorizing—it's intended to be more than a spiritual "common interest." God will lead them into truth, and embracing truth they'll be united, more ready to withstand attack on God's plan for marriage.

▼ *Father, unite us in the wisdom of Your Word.*

FEARS

*The LORD will preserve him and keep
him alive.*
—PS. 41:2

Linda called me wanting my advice on how to handle
a fear her four-year-old was going through. She was
fearing being in front of the audience in a school choir
performance. Linda and her husband didn't want to
overprotect, but they didn't want to press her if she
wasn't ready.

When our son, Eric, was about five, he was going
through a fear of separation from us. He'd gone
through a scary time when we were gone. We also ago-
nized over being too protective. We went through the
pressure of worrying what others would think about us if
we gave in.

The best we could do for Eric was to block out our
own fears of what others thought. We needed to focus
on Eric and what David and I felt was best for our
family.

God "grew" us in our trusting Him with our child.

▼ *Thank You, Father, for walking with us through
every event in our lives.*

WIVES NEED PROTECTION

If anyone does not provide for his own . . .
he . . . is worse than an unbeliever.
　　　　　　　　　　　　　　—1 TIM. 5:8

$\mathcal{A}$lice was constantly "overwhelmed" by home-life pressures. Bill collectors called her daily about overdue bills and bounced checks; the kids demanded her help and attention with activities, school work, quarrels; work claimed her forty hours a week; church activities and her ailing mother claimed her "left-over" time. Her husband, Sam, couldn't imagine why she was so resentful and uninterested in sex. As Sam worked on what it means to protect your wife, Alice found more energy, interest, and romance.

Wives need to feel the protection of husbands, especially in areas of family finances and raising children. Husbands need to be a safe "umbrella" under which wives can take refuge and find support.

 Might I be reminded often of my wife's need for my "umbrella" of protection.

KNOWING WHEN TO PROTECT

Do not forsake [wisdom] and she will preserve you.
—PROV. 4:6

*O*ur one-year-old daughter, Kelly, needs our protection often. She would stick her finger in the wall socket, fall off chairs, climb in the toilet, eat paperclips off the floor, and play in the knife drawer if we didn't protect her from doing so. I like the role of protector in her life.

Spouses also need each other's protection. Sometimes protecting someone can mean loving them enough to stay out of the way and let them do something that will be painful. What they learn will help create wisdom, an internal protection from future harm.

So, I will definitely keep Kelly from sticking her finger in wall sockets, eating paper clips, falling into toilets, and playing in the knife drawer because she needs that kind of protection. With Holly, I will "step in the gap" between her and danger when my doing so is really best for her. I hope she will continue to do the same for me. At other times, though, I will lovingly stay out of the way, praying that God will use the pain to help her gain wisdom.

▼ *God, help me protect my spouse in the ways that are truly helpful and right.*

LEAN ON ME

Spread your protection over them; that those who love your name may rejoice in you.
—PROV. 2:8

$\mathcal{M}$ark, Lesa, and the boys were invited over to her dad's to celebrate her birthday. They arrived an hour later than he had expected. He was furious. He never raised his voice or said an unkind word, but even the children picked up on his unforgiving spirit.

Mark and Lesa apologized and tried to explain, but her father just went about setting the table in cold silence.

Mark was not going to risk the whole evening being ruined. He respectfully told Lesa's father that they would like to stay to celebrate his daughter's birthday with him, but he would not subject his family to this kind of treatment. Her dad would have to make a choice—to talk things over or they were going to leave. Lesa's dad decided to talk, and the evening went well after that.

It was important to Mark to protect his wife from being hurt emotionally.

▼ *God, help me lovingly protect my spouse from harm when it is appropriate for me to do so.*

PROTECTION FROM DRIFTING APART

Guard what was committed to your trust.
—1 TIM. 6:20

Couples sometimes drift apart after several years. We suggest a few ways couples can keep from drifting.

First, we encourage couples to verbalize, to let their spouse know that they miss them, need them, care about them, and appreciate them. Gentle and loving words are soothing, reassuring, and communicate "You're special to me!" Ask about your words: "Can you share with me words that would be meaningful for you to hear?" Ask about actions: "Proverbs 31 speaks about a wife comforting her husband. What can I do to be more comforting to you?" "Ephesians 5 speaks about a husband giving himself up for his wife. How can I demonstrate this to you?" Ask about home atmosphere: "Can you share with me some ideas on what would feel comforting to you?"

Next, we try to lead couples to empathize, to give their spouse the freedom to feel down and to express frustration, anxiety, or fear. Be there with empathetic words and touch. Welcome your spouse home! "Notice" your spouse each evening; initiating contact, smile, touch, communicate you're glad to see your spouse!

▼ *Lord, be for our marriage a great defender and help me to be protective of the love we share.*

REBUKE—TO SET STRAIGHT, REFUTE ERROR, SHARE CONVICTING TRUTH

Preach the word! Be ready in season and out of season. Convince, rebuke, exhort, with all longsuffering and teaching.

—2 TIM. 4:2

*I*f the truth is to "set us free" then the truth must be shared and embraced. Often the needed truth seems unpleasant as wrong is exposed. Often the needed truth seems to hurt, cutting asunder soul from spirit as God's maturing work marches on. God is committed to the truth and will employ any "instrument" in its delivery. For Balaam truth came from a donkey; for Jonah truth was found in a fish; for Peter it came from a dream of unclean animals; and for the prodigal it came in a pen for pigs.

For me, God's rebuke has come through disappointment and defeat; through blocked goals and bounced checks. It's come through health and sleepless nights; and yes, it often comes through the loving but firm words of a caring wife.

▼ *Thanks, Father, for trusting love that risks sharing truth.*

A PRAYER FOR REBUKE

Open rebuke is better
Than love carefully concealed.
—PROV. 27:5

*I*ntimate relationships exist only in openness and flourish only in vulnerability. Holding back truth for fear of rejection or retaliation has no place in an intimate relationship. Given my tendency to "wander," who better to call me back than a caring spouse? Given my vulnerability to deception, who better to remind me of the truth than a loving spouse? Given the work of Christlikeness yet to be completed in me, who better to be the instrument of God's choosing than a sensitive spouse?

▼ *Father, as Your attentive correction is needed, bring across my path the caring spouse You've given me.*

I CAN DO IT MYSELF

*Rebuke is more effective for a wise man
Than a hundred blows on a fool.*
　　　　　—PROV. 17:10

*H*ave you ever been misunderstood? We were to teach a Bible study in Dallas and we were late to the airport. I was only trying to help David find the quickest route. I was only trying to help him find the best spot to park the car. David felt I was trying to take over. After we'd arrived and were going to the restroom, I started to tell him where to set my luggage and he blew up: "I don't need you to tell me how to go to the restroom." My feelings were hurt. When we got to our motel room, I announced, "I don't want to go to the Bible study. Send me home." After David apologized for his part, he shared Romans 8:11, " 'If the Spirit of Him that raised Christ from the dead dwells in you,' Teresa, can't that spirit be in control of your emotions?"

I had to make a choice between my emotions and the truth of that verse. I did go to the Bible study. God was true to His word to bring the feelings when we obey.

▼ *Father, when Your truths rebuke us, we may not like it, but the end is always for our good.*

REBUKE DOES NOT ATTACK

O LORD, do not rebuke me in Your wrath.
—PS. 38:1

*H*oney, I'm concerned that Robin may have been wounded by your impatience with her as you left for work this morning." I was definitely short and irritable as I rushed our daughter out the door. Teresa's words were painful to hear, but mainly because they were true. Nowhere, however, in Teresa's comments was there a personal "attack."

Performance pressure might come in many forms including perfectionism, constant criticism, inappropriate expectations, prideful superiority, endless rules, and social pressure. The demands and resultant criticism might be communicated openly through verbal put-downs, sarcasm, temper rages, and harsh discipline or more subtly through rejection, silence, or withholding. Unlike these actions, loving rebuke encourages change and ministers acceptance.

▼ *Heavenly Father, bring across my path loving rebuke.*

BETTER THAN LOVE CONCEALED

> *Open rebuke is better*
> *Than love carefully concealed.*
> —PROV. 27:5

*L*ove definitely has its "soft" side, but let me suggest it also has its sharp side. Deep love means caring enough to "set somebody straight" when they have driven off the correct path.

We don't like this version of love, and we often refuse to acknowledge it as love when we are on the receiving end. But it is love. Christ told Peter, "Get behind me, Satan," because Peter couldn't accept that Christ had to die. Pretty tough rebuke, but an act of love designed to set Peter back on the path.

Loving our spouses can mean a sharp "setting straight" response to moral error. Doing it right often means making sure you have taken the log out of your own eye first.

▼ *God, help me discern when and how to rebuke my spouse. Help me to be open to loving rebuke.*

GIVE IT TO ME STRAIGHT

The ear that hears the rebukes of life
Will abide among the wise.
—PROV. 15:31

$\mathcal{J}$ remember the outcome of our first marital tiff.

After our argument, Chris shut himself up in his study to get some school work done. I didn't like his doing that, so I packed my suitcase and my lunch for work the next day and trotted off in a huff over to my mother's.

My mom and sister later told me it was all they could do not to laugh out loud when they saw me. Well, I sat down and waited for Chris to discover I was gone and call frantically to see if my mom knew where I was.

An hour passed with no call. So I called him. He couldn't believe I was on the phone. Wasn't I in the bedroom with the door closed? He told me that my going home to Mother's was no solution. We were family now and our problems needed to be kept between us.

What he said was true. Ties with parents need to be replaced with ties between husband and wife. We need to turn to each other to work things out.

▼ *God, please help me to accept being set straight by*
my spouse when I need to be.

REBUKE FROM THE SCRIPTURE

*Having cleansed her by the washing of water
with the word.* —EPH. 5:26 NASB

$\mathcal{M}$ark and Allissa had made great progress in their counseling as hurts were healed, major conflicts eliminated, and friendship restored. Next they desired to tackle their spiritual oneness. Couples often find spiritual closeness through scripture memorization, focusing particularly on passages dealing with marriage, family, and communication. We started them on a joint memory project of ten passages in Proverbs dealing with communication.

We encouraged them to choose a consistent time every day to memorize. They shared in looking up the verse in the Bible and reading the context of the verse. This gives a clearer understanding of the verse as it relates to the thought of that passage. Beginning with the reference, say the reference followed by the verse itself. The verse will normally break down into logical phrases as you take it a phrase at a time until finally you do the whole verse, including the reference. Check each other as you work together saying it aloud.

Mark and Allissa began to use their car-pool time together each morning for their memory work. They quickly had learned over 100 scriptures together, finding fun in correcting each other's slightest mistake!

▼ *Father, hide Your word away in my heart that I
might more fully enjoy You and Your abundance.*

REPROOF—BUILDING UP BY EXPOSING WRONG

Behold, happy is the man whom God corrects.
—JOB 5:17

*G*od's reproof is consistent with His character. He reproves to keep us on the pathway of blessing. He desires not to withhold any good thing from us as we walk uprightly with Him (Ps. 84:11). He not only promises blessings but lovingly reproves to keep us walking toward them! He often "whispers" warning through His still, quiet voice, speaks "audibly" through His Word, and almost "shouts" His plea during many of life's seeming great disappointments.

Marriage without reproof is like an accident waiting to happen. Without the freedom to share truth from a burdened heart, indulgence can go unchecked, selfishness uncorrected, and the entanglements of sin unheeded. God's plan is for caring reproof from a loving spouse.

▼ *Thanks, Father, for Your "check" on my tendency to wander.*

WARNING SIGNS

He who refuses correction goes astray.
—PROV. 10:17

*T*raveling down life's pathway, I come to a fork in the road. Two signs greet me: (1) Receive reproof; (2) go astray. The reproofs are the guardrails of my journey.

Unlike rebuke, reproof is often not spoken but comes through natural consequences, i.e., stay up too late and you're tired the next day. In relationships, reproof comes as needs go unmet in my family members and they seek to meet these needs through others, i.e. a lonely spouse escapes into friendships; a lonely child seeks peer acceptance at any price. As I find a spouse or child turning to others for what God may want me to give them, I find myself at the fork in the road: Will I receive this reproof or go astray? The abundant and intimate marriage receives reproof.

 Help me, Father, to look beyond others' actions and see reproof You have in them for me.

PUSHING MY BUTTONS

The king's heart is in the hand of the LORD,
Like the rivers of water; He turns it wherever
He wishes. —PROV. 21:1

Some of God's most effective reproofs come through
the circumstances of life. I often struggle with wanting to
point out problems and "sins" as if God had assigned
me the Holy Spirit's job!

David often speaks of a man's "macho button," a
mystical place inside a man that recurrent complaining
finally pushes. Then a man begins to rebel: "I wouldn't
change now even if I wanted to!" I finally talked myself
into testing the principle of letting the circumstances of
life teach David.

On our way back from San Antonio I noticed we
needed gas and mentioned it to David. He checked the
other gauge and decided we could go on a few more
miles. When we ran out of gas, I calmly picked up
something to read and told him I hoped he would enjoy
his walk. The theory only had to be tested twice. We've
not run out again.

▼ *Lord, You can change the hearts of kings and hus-*
bands.

REPROOF BALANCES TRUTH WITH LOVE

He will surely rebuke you.
—JOB 13:10

*T*eresa and I are different in so many ways, including how we handle our inevitable marriage hurts. Teresa tends to share the truth, but it might not be in love; my tendency is not to share the truth about my hurt at all. Intimate relationships require that both change: I've become more open; Teresa has become more loving in her expression.

Can I openly and lovingly communicate my needs to my spouse as well as others? Can I discuss my hurts? This is a crucial relationship issue. God instituted marriage, the family, and the church. God often desires to involve "meaningful others" in my life to meet many of my needs. My challenge is to "speak the truth in love" (Eph. 4:15) and then trust God with what He wants to do.

Only with honest and open sharing of needs and hurts can closeness develop. Happy "need" sharing!

▼ *Thanks, Father, for the balance Your Spirit brings to relationships.*

LET ME TURN ON THE LIGHT FOR YOU

*All scripture is given by inspiration of God,
and is profitable for doctrine, for reproof.*
—2 TIM 3:16

*W*e all fall into untruth. It is the human bent to misinterpret, distort, and misperceive reality.

Because we are prone to miss the truth, we all need help seeing it, people who can help "turn on the light."

Now, turning on the light for someone is a delicate thing. There is a certain amount of defensiveness that we all have. it is tough enough being told we aren't thinking right by someone who does it with love and sensitivity, much less by someone who does it hatefully.

Marriage comes into play here. Unfortunately, we show our spouses the error of their mental ways with all the finesse of a bull in a china shop. Hatefully turning on the light drives the spouse further into darkness.

We all miss the truth at times, and we all need help seeing the truth. Our spouses can play a key role in the process of illuminating truth for us, but the goal of our sharing truth needs to be building spouses up, not tearing them down.

▼ *God, help me speak the truth in love so that my
spouse is helped to grow.*

GIVE ME FEEDBACK

Test all things; hold fast what is good.
Abstain from every form of evil.
—1 THESS. 5:21–22

$\mathcal{D}$an was complaining to his wife, Audrey: "I just don't feel close to God. I feel like I do all the right things, perfect Sunday attendance, tithing, and membership on several church committees, but it gets me nowhere. When I pray, I'm not sure He really listens."

Audrey answered, "Dan, close relationships are built by spending lots of time getting to know each other. Two of the best ways I know to do that with God are consistent time spent in Bible study and prayer. If you're like me, you wait to have a quiet time with the Lord until chores are done, dinner is over, and the kids are in bed. He wants more than our lip service; He wants our hearts. For example, prayer would look a lot different than just a wish list for our benefit. It would include praise and thanks to God."

"I think I'm beginning to get it. My perspective needs to change from what can I get from Him to what can I give because He's already given me so much—His Son!"

▼ *Lord, help me to receive feedback from my spouse*
with an open heart.

REPROVING YOUR THOUGHTS AND SPEECH

*If anyone does not stumble in what he says,
he is a perfect man, able to bridle the whole
body as well.* —JAMES 3:2 NASB

Over and over in our counseling work we see signifi-cant maturity take place as couples allow God to chal-lenge and change their self-talk—bringing significant improvements in communication.

A wife innocently declines her husband's invitation to go for a walk. His self-talk says: "She'd go if it were more important to her. Just wait until she asks me to do something with her!" His verbal response may be un-wholesome words: "Never mind, I won't ask again!"

A four-step process helps to control self-talk and im-prove communication. First, *think before you speak—* just because you think something, you don't have to say it! Next comes *taking wrong thoughts "captive"* as you share them with God for Him to empower you to "cast them down" (2 Cor. 10:5). Sharing them with God helps get them out of your system and gives Him time to remind you of the truth. Now the mind is ready to *re-place these thoughts with new ones* that more adequately represent the truth: "My wife is tired or may need time to relax. I know she loves me, and I can use the time alone to think through some personal priorities." Fi-nally, *choose to speak edifying words.* "While I take a walk, why don't you relax or do something you'll enjoy. I'll look forward to our being together when I get back."

▼ *Transform me, Father, by the renewing of my mind.*

RESPECT—CONVEYING GREAT WORTH

He sent his son to them saying, "They will respect my son." . . . But . . . they took him . . . and killed him.   —MATT. 21:37–38

*T*his parable from the lips of Jesus foretold His own betrayal and death. The plea for "respect" would go unheeded. The Father had sent prophets and they were mocked; priests and they were ignored. Surely His people would respect His Son—but not so. Calvary says otherwise. He would come to His own and His own would receive Him not. He would be despised and forsaken among people. He who knew no sin would become sin.

Thus the Godhead understands respect—to value and regard highly, to convey great worth. One day soon the Father will highly exalt His Son, giving Him a name above every other name, that at the name of Jesus every knee shall bow and every tongue confess that *Jesus is Lord!*

▼ *Come, Lord Jesus, come.*

RESPECT AT CALVARY

In honor giving preference to one another.
—ROM. 12:10

*W*ho am I to question the worth or value of one for whom Christ died? Shall the vessel say to the potter: "What is that you've made?" Surely not! There seems to remain only one response and that to affirm and declare the value established at Calvary. But what of this person's sinful behavior and unbelieving heart? What of his ill treatment of me? Is there no justice, no vengeance? The Lord claims vengeance; justice will be measured out by His hand.

Does it not matter that I've been mistreated? Oh yes, it matters much to your Lord. In fact you matter so much and your offender matters so much that there was offered for both of you an unblemished and spotless sacrifice. His name, you ask? Jesus of Nazareth.

 Keep me mindful of my worth, my spouse's worth—both declared by this Jesus.

BURNED MEAT

Let the wife see that she respects her husband.
—EPH. 5:33

*W*hen we were going to have a barbecue for a family get together, David volunteered to do the steaks. He normally lets me do the cooking, so when he volunteered, I doubted his abilities. We had some of our family in the kitchen when I began to tell David how to do the steaks. I wounded him when I didn't respect his abilities. I would never consciously tear him down with my words, but that was exactly what I'd done. I'd shown disrespect for his character and his abilities. Worse still, I'd done it in front of others.

When I realized what I'd done, it really hurt me. I'd shown disrespect out of my own fear. I was fearing what the family would think of the meat. I apologized, asking David to forgive me for the part I'd played in his hurt. I'm so grateful that I became aware of how I hurt David so the hurt could be healed.

▼ *Lord, thank You for Your Spirit that can show me how I've hurt my spouse.*

RESPECT MOTIVATES

When they observe your chaste conduct.
—1 PET. 3:2

During our almost thirty years of marriage, Teresa has faithfully built me up to our children, family, and friends. Her respect for my perspectives and ideas is something I can always count on. She feels free to share her own and at the same time not de-value mine. I never fear her putting me down in front of others. I'm secure that she builds me up to her friends. Such security has often motivated a renewed faithfulness and dedication in my daily walk as husband and father.

Respect is communicated as a helpmate is supportive of her husband's leadership and decisions; respect is fostered as a wife looks to her husband to meet significant needs in her life. Respect is conveyed in a variety of settings—at home, work, church, and social activities.

▼ *Thanks, Father, for the blessing of a respectful wife.*

R-E-S-P-E-C-T, TELL YOU WHAT IT MEANS TO ME

Honor all people.
—1 PET. 2:17

I'm convinced that when you put toilet paper in the toilet paper holder that you should do it so that the sheets come over the top rather than from below. I'm convinced that you should run the vacuum back and forth rather than just straight ahead. I am convinced that the thermostat should be left at 78 in the summer and 68 in the winter. I'm convinced that dishwashers need to be filled to maximum capacity when you do a load. I am convinced that it is much better to get somewhere early than on time. I am convinced you can take a major trip with only one suitcase full of clothes rather than three.

Respect means a lot of different things, but one of the most important is that you regard your spouse's needs and desires just as highly as your own. For marital intimacy to exist, it has to be that way.

▼ *God, help me regard my spouse's ways as highly as my own.*

YOU'RE SOMEONE SPECIAL

A gracious woman retains honor.
—PROV. 11:16

𝒜 new friend, Carol, shared with me today how she and her husband had come to move to this town. They had lived in a wonderful place in Tennessee and were active in their church and community with plenty of dear friends. A job opened up in Texas and her husband very much wanted it. Carol didn't want to move; she saw no need. After much prayer, she felt God encouraging her to put her husband's need for the new job above her own need to stay in Tennessee. By her decision to follow her husband to Texas, she conveyed to him his importance in her eyes. And in response to her obedience, God brought both of them an even fuller, more satisfying life in their new home.

How have you conveyed respect or honor to your spouse? There are thousands of little ways to say you are worth much to me.

 In Your word, Father, You tell me to respect my spouse; show me how to do it in a pleasing way.

RESPECT FOR A FELLOW SAINT

With all respect, not only to those who are good and gentle, but also to those who are unreasonable. —1 PET. 2:18 NASB

*T*eresa and I have noted over the years that discussing what communicates respect is often essential for couples to get on the same wave-length. What communicates respect to one partner may be different for the spouse. We encourage discussing respect and verbalizing needs, which when met enhances the sense of respect.

We work with couples to get them to talk about respect. "In my desire to respect you, your roles, decisions, and leadership, I'd appreciate your sharing with me how I can better communicate my respect." One of the most common responses is that respect is shown when you give feedback privately. If there's question or concern about a decision, lovingly discuss it with your spouse in private.

Next, we help couples explore meaningful needs that when met enhance closeness. Ask yourself, "Why do I need my spouse?" Then verbalize these needs. "It is very special to me when you _____. Thanks."

Finally, we encourage mutual giving, with each partner seeking to give of the self, seeking to communicate a loving respect.

▼ *Father, remind me often of the great worth of Your children, who are joint-heirs with Christ. Might my attitude and behavior be consistent with this divine calling.*

SECURITY—CONFIDENCE OF "HARMONY," FREE FROM HARM

They shall be safe in their land; and they shall know that I am the LORD.
—EZEK. 34:27

*I*t's great to feel confident, free to enjoy life's activities and challenges, confident of supportive, caring relationship. God offers the only true pathway to security: let not a rich man boast in his riches; let not a strong man boast in his chariots; but let him who boasts, boast that He understands and knows God.

Many a couple we've seen has been deceived into thinking security comes from possessions and social status. As marriage separation turns toward divorce, possessions seem to not be enough, and social status is shaken as family and friends "take sides." Genuine security is internal, something of the heart. How thrilling it is to see couples come to experience healing from years of hurt and then see confident security established in one another and with their God.

▼ *Keep me looking to You for my confidence and for my blessing.*

TRUE SECURITY YOU CAN'T EVEN SEE!

Keep sound wisdom and discretion;
Then you will walk safely in your way.
—PROV. 3:21–23

*W*isdom leads to security? Sounds a little strange. You can't touch, count, or even "see" wisdom; how could it possibly bring security? His ways are not our ways; His thoughts are higher than our thoughts. Security comes from within. Couples often look to the number of bedrooms and bathrooms as a testimony of security. Couples have relied on their "immunity" against divorce as their security. Man builds walls, armies, and bank accounts seeking security. God builds a person to relate intimately with Himself, then with loved ones around him.

The growing confidence that my Creator can be trusted deepens my security in Him. The growing confidence that my spouse can be trusted deepens my marriage security and intimacy.

▼ *Father, keep me walking according to the things that cannot be seen.*

MORE THAN A ROOF OVER MY HEAD

Shall I not seek security for you.
—REV. 3:1

My feeling secure does not come from David's putting in burglar alarms, putting better locks on doors, or keeping me from bodily harm. To me security comes if David makes sure the lights are off, the alarm is set, and the locks are locked. To some security may mean taking care of the bills or interceding with a parent. In other words, security is different for everyone.

A lot of my security needs feel like things my dad did for us. I can't expect David to be my dad because some things David can do and some things he can't. I need to get below the visible actions and see what I need in order to feel secure. To feel really secure I need to sense that he wants to protect me, that he notices what hurts me. Sometimes I need to let David know what he can do to help me feel more secure. I can't expect him to know everything I need; only when I express those needs can he fulfill them.

▼ *Father, my security must be in You first.*

ME, INSECURE?

*Who can find a virtuous wife? . . . The heart
of her husband safely trusts her.*
—PROV. 31:10–11

A common occurrence is the "mystery" of a man's
insecurity. Men are typically conditioned to act tough
and self-reliant, to resist emotional expression and
never admit weakness. All such behaviors hinder intimacy. Underneath all this exterior image is often a fearful, insecure "little boy," needful of a wife's reassuring
love.

Security speaks of an inner confidence that is certain
and sure: a husband comes to have this deep confidence as trust in him is exhibited and commitment to
him is expressed. Trust in him is often deepened as a
wife helps cast out his fears through verbalized reassurance and initiated affection; commitment to him is often
communicated through genuine support and sincere
praise.

▼ *I'm grateful, Father, for the reassuring love of a
faithful wife.*

ME AND MY COPILOT

His heart is established;
He will not be afraid.
—PS. 112:8

I am convinced my wife has "stealth" capabilities when we go shopping. We can enter a department store at the same time, walk into the same section of the store, and she disappears. She's there, but she's not there.

Until I find her, I don't feel quite right. My "copilot" is missing, if you know what I mean.

Marriage is supposed to be like that. We are supposed to feel somewhat uncomfortable when apart from our spouses because they are our copilots while we are down here on earth. We fly the same plane together, and there is less security in flying alone.

My wife's "stealth" capabilities in a department store can be frustrating, but they call up that part of me that knows she is important.

God is the ultimate pilot of our lives and our only true source of security. Yet in a committed marriage relationship, He gives us an earthly taste of our security in Him.

▼ *God, thank You for blessing me with a copilot.*

DO YOU HAVE A SECURITY BLANKET?

> *The beloved of the LORD shall*
> *dwell in safety by Him,*
> *Who shelters him all the day long.*
> —DEUT. 33:12

*E*ach of our children, as babies, had a special something to take to bed each night as "security."

Our son, Matthew, took one of my hair rollers; our daughter, Ashley, took the same baby blanket to snuggle with; and Kelly Ann, our one-year-old, takes two pacifiers, one for her mouth and the other to hold. At night, if we heard crying or even restlessness, there was a good chance their prize possession had fallen out of their reach. As soon as we returned it to them they settled back down and fell asleep.

Remembering all this made me think of Chris and how he gives me security. His physical presence reassures me that I am loved and safe. I still have that security.

Because God knows your need for security and wants to meet it, He often will create in marriage a safe haven away from the outside would.

▼ *Thank You that I am secure in You, Lord. Help me to create a safe place in my marriage.*

FREE FROM FEAR'S CONTROL

God has not given us a spirit of fear.
—2 TIM. 1:7

*F*ear of the future robs couples of present fulfillment. We often encourage couples to begin addressing their fears openly through verbalizing, prioritizing, and mutual accountability.

First, we teach verbalizing skills when dealing with fears. They may say, "Honey, could you share some of the things you've been worrying about or fearing? I'd like to help you with them." Learn to ask about fears and security. "What could I do to help you feel more secure in our relationship?"

Second, we challenge couples to make sure they consistently prioritize their relationship through regularly scheduled couple dates—doing something for fun, without children (that's family time), and without friends (that's social time). Having scheduled dates offers the security of a vital relationship.

Third, we encourage couples to develop mutual accountability. Ask each other: "What are some things I've been doing recently that irritate you? I want to work on changing them." Listen attentively without defensiveness; pray about what is shared and implement needed changes. A willingness to consider a partner's wishes for change helps deepen security in the relationship.

 Manifest Your love through me, Father, that it might cast out all fear.

SERVE—GIVING TO EACH OTHER

Through love serve one another.
—GAL. 5:13

*T*rue "serving" springs forth from a selfless, loving motive. There's much labeled as "serving" in our day which is not. Activity which calls attention to oneself is not serving. Involvement in "helping" others as a social opportunity to be well "thought of" is not serving. Giving to others less fortunate from a guilt-ridden heart is not serving. Caring for another in order that they'll "care" for me is manipulation, not serving.

Serving another comes from the overflow of a heart filled with wonderment that I've been served by the carpenter from Nazareth. He who had everything left it all in my behalf. He who could have called ten thousand angels to serve Him at the cross chose instead to serve me.

▼ *Might the awe and wonder of His gift to me prompt loving service to others near me.*

CHRIST OUR ROLE MODEL

The Son of Man did not come to be served, but to serve.
—MATT. 20:28

*W*hat a role model! If there was ever one who deserved to be treated special it was He. Rather than focus on what He deserved, He seemed to live reminded of who He was and all that was His. From this identity and inheritance a grateful giving in the service of others springs forth.

I wonder if it would work for me? I wonder if fully understanding who I am would overflow my heart with grateful giving? I wonder if fully appreciating my inheritance in Him would prompt sensitive caring for others? So what does my God say about me and my inheritance? I am a beloved child of God, blessed with everything pertaining to life and Godliness! I guess we'll see if it can prompt the miracle of serving others—beginning in my marriage.

 Teach me, Father, who I really am and what I've really received.

WHEN IS IT MY TURN?

It is the Lord Christ whom you serve.
—COL. 3:24 NASB

$\mathcal{D}$avid used to walk in the house from work with his hand up like he was holding a glass. That was his way of saying, "I need a glass of tea. I've had a really hard day."

Today, with both partners working, the woman may feel like asking "When will I be served? I've had a hard day, too."

Our counsel is consistently the same whether it's with the husband, the wife, or both. Someone needs to start giving as they lovingly serve the other, trusting God with their own needs.

First, I need to start giving even though my spouse isn't simply because God has already given to me. Second, serving my spouse must be done lovingly with joy—obviously not with anger and resentment. Third, when I find myself growing weary in serving another, it's important to lovingly share my needs with my spouse and then trust God with the results. God can be counted on to work in my partner's life or to minister to me through avenues of His choosing.

When I find myself growing weary in serving, it's important to review these three reflections and allow God to speak to me about my part.

 Father, each of us must give an account to You only for ourselves. I want to be faithful in my part.

FREE TO SERVE

What I will to do, that I do not practice.
—ROM. 7:15

*T*eresa needed me to "give" lovingly to her when we married, but it didn't often happen. She needed me to prioritize serving her in special ways but I rarely did so. I made many apologies and recommitments, but they were short lived. I identified with the apostle Paul in his Romans 7 dilemma: "The good that I will to do, I do not do; but the evil I will not to do, that I practice" (v. 19). I wasn't "free" to love; unresolved issues in my own life held me captive in selfish preoccupation. God began a slow but productive liberating work. God comforted and ministered grace. Freedom to give and serve Teresa followed.

Intimacy involves a freedom to share all of oneself—body, soul, and spirit—with your spouse. A wife needs a husband who is experiencing a growing personal freedom and is involved in encouraging her freedom; in a similar way he is committed to serving and giving, not taking.

▼ *Father, thanks for freedom from above.*

HOW GOOD IS YOUR SERVE?

With good will doing service, as to the Lord, and not to men.
—EPH. 6:7

*H*ave you ever found yourself "greenstamping" your spouse, doing something for them but internally deciding they owe you for it? Unfortunately, I do it all the time.

The other day I was changing a particularly nasty diaper. As the smell hit me, I thought, "Holly really owes me for this one!"

We freely choose to do the things we do in marriage, yet we think we are owed some kind of payback for it. The only type of marriage that really works is "100-100"—we both do what needs to be done to make our marriage work.

The human bent is to do things to get some kind of payoff. But marital intimacy is destroyed by a "greenstamp" mind-set.

Intimacy in marriage is impossible if you are "greenstamping" your spouse. Seek to serve, not to be served.

▼ *God, help me to develop a servant's heart toward my spouse.*

ASPIRIN ANYONE?

*If anyone ministers, let him do it as with the
ability which God supplies, that in all things
God may be glorified through Jesus Christ.*
—1 PET. 4:11

$\mathcal{I}$n my childhood home being sick was always a big
deal—lots of attention, games, special food and service.
In Chris's family illness was an inconvenience to be ignored.

When we were first married and Chris became ill I
tried to badger him into lying down and eating some
soup. He hated the fuss. When I got sick I naturally
assumed he would lovingly take care of me. Instead
he'd say, "If you stay active, you'll feel better."

Fortunately God has brought us a long way since
then. I've stopped trying to baby him, and he's responded by letting me get him a few things like medi-
cine or a drink. And Chris has become much more
sympathetic to my need for time to rest away from the
kids.

God showed us both that being a good servant is listening to the needs of your spouse.

▼ *Lord, help me to ask how I can best serve my
spouse's needs; give me patience and discernment.*

SERVING EACH OTHER

*So that we should serve in the newness of
the Spirit.*   —ROM. 7:6

*M*utual giving is one of the goals we work for in our counseling. As each marriage partner finds freedom and motivation to serve the other, intimacy follows. Caring for another during life's endless demands is what a servant's heart is all about. Serving another person is most often in the daily considerations and not necessarily "big" things.

First, we encourage couples to ask about wishes. "Honey, I honestly want to better honor you as my partner. Would you share with me some wishes that I could help fulfill?" Listen attentively, then lovingly give!

Next, we might challenge the couple to talk about decisions. "As I come to realize how much I need and value your wisdom, I want to become more sensitive to your opinions. Can you share with me decision areas in which you'd appreciate more support?" This helps to bring more oneness and less tension into the decision-making process.

Another area we explore is teaching them not to sweat the small stuff! Let your spouse make decisions and even mistakes. Let him or her miss an exit off the expressway or pick a restaurant with a long waiting line; let her or him verbalize "wild" ideas without shooting them down! Sometimes we serve another by our silence.

▼ *Father, free us for serving each other.*

SUPPORT—HELPING CARRY BURDENS

And Aaron and Hur supported his hands,
one on one side, and the other on the other
side; and his hands were steady.
—EX. 17:12

*T*he armies of the Lord prevailed against the enemy as Aaron and Hur provided support. Joshua led the Israelites into battle as Moses stood with the rod of God outstretched over the valley below. As the rod was lifted up, Joshua and the Israelites prevailed, but when Moses grew tired and the rod was lowered, the enemies prevailed. Aaron and Hur noticed the need and came to render support; no plea was made for them to come, but they took the initiative.

That's the way it is with true support—noticing needs, taking initiative, quietly giving of oneself. It took me several years to move past seeing only my need, to finally notice Teresa's. But recent years have been exciting and fulfilling as needs are noticed, initiative taken, and support given.

▼ *Help me, Lord, to lift up my partner.*

THE JOY OF MUTUAL SUPPORT

It is more blessed to give than to receive.
—ACTS 20:35

*I*t's been humorous to find Teresa and myself in "conflict" over who gives to whom, who serves whom. It hasn't always been that way, but it's a joy to see the blessing of mutual giving. For many years I would never have understood or believed that it was better to give than to receive—but it really is!

Giving to one another characterizes a healthy relationship. Both have received of God's abundance, and they now "freely give (Matt. 10:8). When a compliment is shared, it is prompted by genuine appreciation, not intended to manipulate.

All the ways of a man are pure in his own eyes
But the LORD weighs the spirits.

(Prov. 16:2)

God will honor a motive of "giving" as intimacy is deepened and relational abundance is experienced.

▼ *Lord, it's a miracle that I've first received from You, and it's now a joy and privilege to give.*

WITH ME ALL THE WAY

I am with you always.
—MATT. 28:20

$\mathcal{I}$ was giving a new message to a women's conference in the Houston area. New messages always make me nervous.

David had volunteered to drive me since I couldn't fly to the retreat ground. We were almost an hour down the road when I pulled out my messages to review for the weekend and realized I'd left the new message on the desk. David was so supportive, he offered to take me on to the retreat and then return to Austin and get my notes. I've never felt so much support from anyone. It felt so good to know that he would go that much out of his way to support me. We stopped and called a friend to meet us halfway with my notes and then called to let the women at the retreat know that I was on the way. The support from David was an example to me of how I could be a support to him in the future.

 Father, thank You for giving us Your Spirit to support us all the way.

THE MIRACLE OF MUTUAL GIVING

Bear one another's burdens and so fulfill the law of Christ.
—GAL. 6:2

*N*otice that we have both the command to bear burdens and the privilege to share them. There are not some "bearers" and others who are "bearees." We easily grow weary in doing good when we're always "bearing" and never sharing with others. We have the opportunity to bear the burdens of others around us, the common life struggles of sadness, defeat, temptation, and despair. We also have the privilege of allowing others to get close enough to join us in bearing our burdens.

This truth argues loudly for the vulnerability that is vital in an intimate marriage, a willingness to admit need, share struggles, and receive support. Couples can journey through healing hurts, gaining freedom, and finally mutual giving, each joyfully giving to the intimacy needs of the other.

▼ *Lord, whatever it takes, heal us and free us for mutual giving.*

LEARNING TO DRIVE

*Come to me all you who labor and are heavy
laden, and I will give you rest.*
                                        —MATT. 11:28

*C*an you imagine going over to England for the first
time and trying to learn to drive on the left side of the
road? I wonder what it would be like to approach a
busy, downtown intersection in London.

Marriage can be like learning to drive on the left side
of the road. We are learning a whole new set of "driving" skills.

Because marital intimacy is so difficult to learn, we
really need to support each other. Most of us feel pretty
lost and awkward in our efforts to learn how to be intimate, so we don't need someone putting us down. In
fact, the more they put us down, the less we want to try
to be close.

Support your spouse—they are learning to drive on
the left side of the road. They will need a lot of love,
understanding, and patience from you.

▼ *God, help me to support my spouse in learning how
to be an intimate partner.*

I'M FALLING

For my yoke is easy and my burden is light.
—MATT. 11:30

*T*hey had worked and prayed for this promotion for ten years now. At last her husband had been chosen as the vice-president of the biggest computer company in their city. Yes, they had made sacrifices along the way, especially in family time. But it had been worth it, hadn't it?

Then their world came crashing down, their sixteen-year-old son was arrested for breaking into a pharmacy, looking for drugs. Thankfully he was put on two year's probation and enrolled in a drub rehab program.

Her husband came home early one evening to talk to her. God had convicted him of how out of balance his life had become. He wanted to quit and get a less demanding job, maybe even in a smaller town. Start all over again. He wanted control of his life back. Would she support his decision? Would she help him learn how to be a husband and a father again? How could she refuse? She loved him.

In marriage we are to bear each other's burdens.

▼ *Lord, give me the sensitivity always to seek to share in my spouse's struggles.*

SUPPORTING THE LOAD

*Bear one another's burdens, and so fulfill the
law of Christ.* —GAL. 6:2

*T*empers often flair when we reach overload. Supporting your spouse helps reduce the tension, encourages mutual sharing, and magnifies feelings of love.

In our "preventative" counseling, we help couples develop a strategy for handling inevitable stress, determining what things overwhelm their partner—too little money, too many kids, too little privacy. When you sense marital conflict approaching, ask yourself: "Is my spouse reacting out of feeling overwhelmed?" If so, address this feeling with understanding, empathy, and possibly confession/forgiveness. It might be helpful to ask, "I want to better protect you from highly stressful times and feelings. Can you share with me how I might do this?"

Another dimension of support is to have times of "escape." Lovingly insist and then support your partner's occasional "escape" into something fun—lunch with friends, reading a book, window shopping—just for fun.

Finally, couple prayer times are important. After talking about an area of concern, hold hands and pray. You'll sense God's spiritual protection.

▼ *Father, sensitize me to my partner's warning signs of overload. Bring me alongside to lovingly help.*

SYMPATHY—IDENTIFYING WITH EACH OTHER "EMOTIONALLY"

Jesus wept.
—JOHN 11:35

*T*he son of man enters into the emotional pain surrounding the death of His friend Lazarus. Consistently across the pages of Scripture we see an involved and sensitive Savior. He's there to enter into the loneliness of a tax collector, the rejection of a leper, or the helpless feeling of a rejected child. But why does He? It's not His divinity that requires such involvement, but rather His humanity. If He's to be our great High Priest, He must enter into our emotional world of joy and pain, victory and grief.

Couples we see in marriage difficulty have for prolonged periods of time remained detached and withdrawn from their partner's pain. They may have analyzed, escaped, rationalized, or blamed but resisted entering into the emotional pain of another. Our counseling journey leads them together into this valley, most often to find the joy of sensing that someone cares!

▼ *Father, lead me into my partner's emotional world— to care, to love.*

THE MYSTERY OF ONENESS

All of you be of one mind, having compassion.
—1 PET. 3:8

*H*armony and sympathy come from a sense of feeling connected to another person; bonded, attached. Scripture speaks of Christians being part of one body with Christ as the head (1 Cor. 12), the Holy Spirit having connected us to one another. We care, therefore, when another is sad or hurt. The Bible says that in marriage two become "one." As this mystical oneness deepens, each partner becomes increasingly sensitive to the emotions of the other. Being understood and identified with emotionally are key ingredients in marital intimacy.

This mystery of connectedness is one of the key reasons we do most of our marriage counseling in sessions with both partners present. How can we help one partner when the "other half" is not present? It's also our view that God intends for each spouse to play a vital role in the therapy. A spouse's verbalized appreciation will mean more to the partner than a counselor's will. Empathy from a spouse will touch deeper than a mere counselor's.

▼ *Help us, Father, with the mystery of two becoming one.*

I WANT MY MOMMY

No one comforts me.
—LAM. 1:21

The preschoolers in Bible study were out on the playground when one little girl just barely nicked her finger. One of the teachers tried to tell her that she wasn't hurt badly, that her finger would quit hurting soon. But the child didn't believe it; she just kept crying.

I picked her up and started talking to her about her finger and how bad it must be hurting her. When I asked her if she wanted her mom, she responded anxiously. We talked about wanting Mommy until her mother came. The little girl was then fine.

We are not taught how to give sympathy, but we all need it. Sympathy is not facts or reasons. Sympathy is talking to me about my pain. We adults can feel just like the little girl in her pain; she just wanted the one she loved to give her sympathy over her hurt.

▼ *Lord, You've felt sympathy for us ever since creation. Thank You for Your compassion.*

NOT SATISFIED WITH COPING

If you do well, will not your countenance be lifted up?
—GEN. 4:7 NASB

*P*hilip came for counseling by himself, describing depressive symptoms, related to his marriage. He was embarrassed for being depressed and having marriage problems, especially since he was a Christian. He was tired of pretending that everything was okay.

As for Philip and many couples, this coping existence is made even more tragic by its contrast with religious expectations and hopes. Much pretending takes place as what is observed at home is so different from what is proclaimed at church. Can I genuinely be living consistent with the grace of God's forgiveness while at the same time harboring anger and bitterness toward my spouse? When a person's home life is dramatically different from his or her spiritual values and teachings, feelings of inadequacy, guilt, and condemnation are often added to the previous pain of loneliness, rejection, fear, anger, or bitterness.

We helped Philip to explore unresolved anger, which was contributing to his depression. It had not been helpful for him to simply recommit to not being angry at his wife. We identified the hurt underneath his anger and involved his wife for a meaningful time of forgiveness and comfort. Healing was underway; coping began to give way to abundance.

▼ *Thanks, Father, for Your promise of abundance.*

A WHALE OF A STORY

You had compassion on me.
—HEB. 10:34

*H*olly and I celebrated our tenth anniversary on Maui, Hawaii. Talk about an incredibly beautiful place! God really pulled off a masterpiece when He made Maui.

We decided to go whale watching. So we and about ten other tourists climbed into a motorized rubber raft and took off into the ocean to get up close and personal with some whales.

About five minutes into the trip, the up-and-down bumping and banging of the rubber raft made me sicker than a dog.

Holly grabbed my hand, asked how she could help, got me a soft drink, and asked the other people on the ride if they had any seasickness medication.

That is what marriage is supposed to be like. When you feel your worst, your spouse pulls alongside you and offers to help.

By the way, the closest we got to a whale was about three hundred yards. But what Holly did that day was worth it.

 God, help me walk inside my spouse's shoes and sympathize with her/his pain.

I HURT WHEN YOU HURT

For You have delivered . . .
My eyes from tears,
My feet from falling.
—PS. 116:8

I was in a parking lot getting ready to reenter street traffic. My kids were in the back seat, and my friend Kathy was up front with me. I saw a van's back-up lights come on as I glanced over my shoulder. The man driving didn't seem to know we were behind him. We could only watch as he ran his car into mine.

Almost in tears, I got out to look at the damage. The man in the van admitted his carelessness and apologized, but all I could see was the bashed-in car door. I felt I had let Chris down even though the accident wasn't my fault.

Before I reached the back door, Chris came running out and gave me a reassuring hug. He told me Kathy had called with the news about the accident after I dropped her off. He knew I must be feeling pretty bad, but he encouraged me not to. He reminded me it wasn't my fault, and anyway the kids and I were most important. Chris's sympathetic reaction that day almost made me glad the accident had happened.

 God, help my spouse and me to understand each other's feelings.

FAMILY NIGHT "FEELING" PROJECT

And they made an appointment together to come to sympathize with him and comfort him.
—JOB 2:11 NASB

$\mathcal{I}$t's not uncommon for us to encounter couples struggling with the lack of emotional closeness. One of the first challenges is to develop a vocabulary of feelings. It's impossible to be vulnerable in sharing feelings when we don't know what to call them!

We encouraged Don and Margaret to begin a "feeling chart." They purchased a poster board and divided it into two columns for "Positive" and "Negative" feelings. The entire family participated in naming as many feelings as possible. We challenged them to try to name 15–20 positive and 15–20 negative feelings, remembering that "negative" doesn't mean "wrong." After a few nights of developing a feeling vocabulary, they were ready to move on to sharing feelings.

Don and Margaret and the kids were now ready to take turns for several nights sharing an event that happened that day and how it made them feel. Each family member shared a positive event/feeling and then a negative one. This project can make a major contribution to validating that it's okay to feel and to talk about feelings. Imagine the impact on a child who hears that Dad felt lonely or sad; the child concluded that it must be okay to feel lonely or sad!

▼ *Thanks, Lord, that You're a "feeling" God, able to sympathize as our great High Priest.*

TEACHING—CONSTRUCTIVE LIFE INSTRUCTION

Teach me Your way, O Lord.
—PS. 27:11

*E*ach of us is a mere student, uninformed and ill prepared for life. There's none of us who sees beyond the present moment to what really lies ahead. There's none who can ever calculate the full implications of any decision. There's a painful sense of finitude about such realizations, reminders of my mere humanity. Maybe it was such thoughts that prompted the psalmist to cry out: "Teach me Your ways, O Lord."

I've observed another dimension of these reflections. Even when I've made the decision, thinking surely it's best, it often brings a disappointing outcome. At other times, I've demanded "my way" and it's found tragic results. At still others, the very things I don't want to choose, I keep choosing as if I'm programmed to go "my way." Maybe this was also a part of the psalmist's cry.

▼ *Teach me Your ways, O Lord. I need them!*

MARRIAGE BUILT ON SOLID ROCK

*Let the word of Christ dwell in you richly in
all wisdom, teaching . . . one another.*
—COL. 3:16

*L*ife, marriage, and family are being lived from some
set of standards. My standards may come from TV or
peer pressure, but some set of values and priorities is
being used for guidance. The Scriptures give me a
foundation upon which to base decisions, a "grid"
through which I view life's issues. Here is the solid
rock . . . all other standards are sinking sand.

A reflective sharing of personal insights derived from
the Scripture is good. We recommend devotional reading of a chapter in Proverbs each day of the month,
taking opportunity to share highlights at the dinner table. This sharing can deepen a couple's sense of spiritual intimacy and can provide a great testimony to the
always watchful eyes of children.

 *Bring us often together, Father, around the truth
from Your Word.*

GET OUT YOUR PAD AND PENCIL!

My son, do not forget my teaching.
—PROV. 3:1 NASB

*D*avid's spiritual gift is teaching. He loves to study, prepare, write, and then teach what God has shown him. When the kids were young, David tried to "talk" to them about issues in their lives that needed correction. Instead of being concise, he "taught" them.

One day in one of our family times, the kids asked David a simple question that required a simple answer. When David started into a long answer, one of the kids burst out, "Oh, no! Get out your pad and pencil. Dad's gonna teach."

We've laughed often about that comment, but our family and others outside the family admire and appreciate David's ability to impart God's Word. David's ability to teach God's Word has been a great comfort to me. I've known I could always turn to him to help me know where to go for answers in God's Word.

▼ *Lord, thank You for a husband who has a desire for Your Word.*

TEACH ME TO RECEIVE

*I, therefore . . . entreat you to walk in a
manner worthy of the calling with which you
have been called.* —EPH. 4:1 NASB

"Tell me what I need to do to get my wife back," Allen
said in our first session. I had been seeing his wife,
Jeannie, for several months and knew that Allen had
been trying hard. He had sent flowers and gifts and quit
golfing to be home in case Jeannie called. As I listened
to Allen I remembered Jeannie's words to me: "I've
just needed Allen to accept me the way I am, to quit
trying to make me like him." Allen had been trying
hard, doing things while Jeannie needed him to "be"
someone—an accepting someone!

The world tends to operate on the premise of doing
things in order to be okay. We work too hard to get
raises, but working hard can't make us okay with God
(Titus 3:5); it becomes a performance trap as it hinders
relationships with others. Intimate relationships are
founded upon first being accepted, loved, and valued.
Then follows a desire to do things consistent with this
acceptance, love, and worth.

We had the privilege of leading Allen into the inexpressible joy of receiving Christ. He struggled with the
fact that he could do nothing to merit Christ but needed
simply to receive Him. And Christ's acceptance soon
found its way in expression to Jeannie. God had been
the Great Physician to heal their marriage.

▼ *Lord, it's a blessing to receive from You and then
have the joyful privilege of sharing.*

"HOW ARE YOUR GRADES?"

In doctrine showing integrity, reverence, . . .
sound speech that cannot be condemned.
—TITUS 2:7

*M*y two older children came home with fantastic report cards the other day. The kids wanted to know how I was prepared to reward them. They suggested a trip to DisneyWorld. We are still negotiating, especially since I thought a trip to the local pizza parlor might be enough.

It got me to thinking about my own "report card" as a spouse. How would I grade out? We are all in the classroom each day. We are taking Intimacy 101, and it is one of the toughest classes we will ever take. Sometimes we teach our spouses; sometimes our spouses teach us. All the time, God is the senior teacher.

We may have a lot more in common with our children than we realize.

▼ *God, help me lovingly teach and learn from my spouse.*

YOU'RE NEVER TOO OLD TO LEARN

*Speak the things which are proper for sound
doctrine.*
                                    —TITUS 2:1

*W*e were out having dinner with some dear friends. I complimented Roberta on her talk that morning at the Bible study. She downplayed what she had done.

Bob, her husband, interrupted. "Now, honey, what should we be saying instead?" She looked from him back to us and said, "Thank you, Holly. So nice of you to notice." Bob explained he was helping Berta to learn to accept praise. Since Chris and I struggle with receiving compliments, we decided to adopt this strategy.

We began to see just how often we stiff-armed compliments. Soon we found ourselves passing along what we had learned from our friends about how to accept praise.

There are a lot of different ways to teach. Perhaps the best is through example. Our friends taught us something important through their actions toward each other.

What are you teaching other couples who are watching your marriage?

▼ *God, help my spouse and me to learn from what other couples have to teach us.*

THE TEACHING POWER OF MEDITATION

Man shall not live by bread alone, but by every word that proceeds from the mouth of God.
—MATT. 4:4

*F*or couples desiring to deepen their spiritual growth together, memorizing all of 1 Corinthians 13 is an assignment we might give in counseling. This "Love Chapter" is filled with God's teaching on the characteristics of divine love; hiding it away in your heart helps make the reality of it a lot closer! Couples also benefit from memorizing scripture passages that directly speak to their needs; not only individual verses, but large passages of scripture are important. Try James 1, Matthew 5—7, Hebrews 12, John 15, Colossians 3, and Romans 5—8.

We then encourage couples to "personalize" the passage. God delights to hear His own word, especially when we use it to express our own desires and emotions. To do this, take the sections you memorized and add personal pronouns wherever possible. Turning these passages into mental pictures helps to visualize the truth and turn memorization into meditation. Choosing to dwell on scriptural pictures of God's truth can give us sustained victory in our thought life. We can learn to build these mental pictures of key truths by rehearsing in our mind what patience or kindness might look like, helping to remind us of what true love is.

▼ *Nourish me from Your truth, O Lord.*

TOLERANCE—PATIENT ENDURANCE
OF ANOTHER'S HUMANNESS

With all lowliness and gentleness, with longsuffering, bearing with one another in love.
—EPH. 4:2

*V*ery bluntly, tolerance relates to putting up with another person's obvious humanness, forbearing with them in their imperfections. Humans are peculiar, and spouses sometimes seem the strangest of the lot! These peculiarities seem to be especially centered around how different people are from *me*. Somehow I see myself as the norm.

To express tolerance demands setting aside this self-centered focus on myself and adopting instead a God-centered perspective as He sees each of us as very different, peculiar, and "strange!" As God patiently works this truth into my life, tolerance has had many payoffs: more patience, less anxiety, more fun, less conflict, even lower blood pressure!

▼ *Thank You, Father, for Your powerful example in putting up with me . . . and my weirdness.*

GRACE IS TOLERANT

For by grace you have been saved.
—EPH. 2:8

*H*ow can I put up with his sloppiness?" "How can I keep overlooking her being late?" Couples in our sessions often ask how they can possibly keep tolerating their partners' faults and weaknesses. And I often think to myself, "You can give up on them as soon as God does—never!" Who among us is not being "tolerated" by our Creator, having benefited from His gracious tolerance? This gift frees us to accept and love others unconditionally.

Unconditional love "frees" a spouse from performing in order to please. Having partaken of grace, I'm genuinely free to give to others. "Freely you have received, freely give" (Matt. 10:8).

Having received what I could not earn and did not deserve, I'm free from the fear of never having it and the fear of ever losing it. This liberty of gracious acceptance builds intimacy. In this freedom, tolerance of my spouse comes easily.

▼ *Thanks, Lord, for Your tolerance of me.*

I'LL NOT BE YOUR MOTHER!

Or how can you say to your brother,
"Brother, let me remove the speck that
is in your eye," when you yourself do
not see the plank that is in your own eye?
—LUKE 6:42

$\mathcal{O}$ne of the "sins" in David's life is being late. He's been late ever since we were first married. I used to get so upset, I'd be uptight and cranky before we even left to go anywhere. When we arrived, I'd be embarrassed and feel I needed to make excuses for us.

I began to see the sins in my life as God sees them. I began to see my responsibility in how I was letting David's actions cause me to sin. My attitude over David's being late was a sin against God. When I examined the plank in my own eye, I could be more tolerant of David's "sin."

It is so freeing now to realize I'm not responsible *for* my husband. When I nag over his being late or try to cover for him, I'm mothering. God didn't call me to be a mother to David. He called me to be a wife.

▼ *God, when You see the need to change my spouse,*
You change him.

CAN I RESENT TOLERATING YOU?

Bearing with one another, and forgiving one another . . . even as Christ.

—COL. 3:13

*T*he Lord is the ultimate example of tolerance. He who is perfect, holy, and complete puts up with me, imperfect, sinful, and incomplete. God doesn't resent tolerating me; He doesn't pout and act like a martyr while He waits for me to "grow up." He's kind, gentle, and patiently loving. He must know I'll "arrive" one day, even if it is in the world to come. I wonder if I could have this attitude toward my spouse: realizing that when He appears, she shall be like Him? As God has tolerated me and continues to do so, maybe I can tolerate Teresa's imperfections?

It seems like the more I've grown to understand and appreciate God's tolerance of me, the more I've had available for Teresa.

▼ *Lord, I'm grateful for Your longsuffering over me.*

"BITE YOUR THUMB"

Love suffers long.
—1 COR. 13:4

*M*y family used to vacation to various places by car. My parents put a cooler of soft drinks in the car to keep my brothers and me pacified during the trips.

The only problem was that we often drank so many soft drinks that we needed to go to the bathroom every thirty minutes or so. On one trip, we boys were all raising a fuss about the need to stop for another bathroom break. My dad finally turned around to us in the back seat and said, with a grin on his face, "Bite your thumb."

In marriage, too, we often are required to endure, patiently tolerating an annoying habit or personality characteristic. We all have these, so we all need tolerance from our spouses.

▼ *God, help me be tolerant toward my spouse, patiently enduring what is difficult or challenging.*

I LOVE YOU ANYWAY

Uphold the weak, be patient with all.
—1 THESS. 5:14

$\mathcal{I}$ get lost a lot. It's so easy for me to get turned around, and I can't make heads or tails out of a map.

While I was driving my mom from Oklahoma to Texas, we talked and enjoyed the scenery, evidently a little too much because we ended up in Arkansas. Chris, on the other hand, never gets lost. He seems to intuitively know where he's going.

Recently we were looking for some friends' apartment complex. I'd been there once before a couple of weeks earlier. I didn't remember exactly where the complex was, but I was sure I'd recognize it when I saw it. We tried one complex; then we tried another. "Maybe we could go just a little farther," I suggested.

Chris was frustrated. But he did not attack me or my character. Instead, he suggested we stop, call our friends, and get directions. He was showing tolerance.

▼ *God, please help my spouse and me to be tolerant of each other's styles, no matter how irritating they may be.*

BUILD TOLERANCE THROUGH GRATITUDE

Forget none of His benefits.
—PS. 103:2 NASB

*F*rances and Derrick were impatient with each other, lacking any tolerance for differences of perspective or opinion. After working on several underlying issues we returned to this in one of our subsequent sessions. Particularly I emphasized that tolerance is developed through re-focusing on a partner's strengths. If all I see are Teresa's faults, my patience is often little. Deepening my gratefulness helps me to look beyond irritations and weaknesses as they are observed.

Frances and Derrick discussed some of the benefits of a grateful heart. They noted that gratitude guards us from a critical, negative attitude; it guards us from a judgmental spirit, and, when expressed, can encourage others to continue in "good deeds." Gratitude, when acknowledged to God, is an important element of worship.

In applying these insights to their marriage, we encouraged them to re-discover areas of appreciation, considering some of the reasons they were originally attracted to each other. They found that many of these qualities still existed but had been taken for granted. Additionally, we challenged them to discover areas of appreciation, reflecting on their own limitations or weaknesses to see if each had many "compensating" qualities the other appreciated.

▼ *Remind me often of the special blessing I've received in the gift of marriage.*

TRAINING—JOURNEY WITH ME TO MODEL GOD'S WAY OF FACING LIFE

Everyone who is perfectly trained will be like his teacher.
—LUKE 6:40

*E*ver wonder why people are so often anxious? Anxiety is common in individuals and marriages today. There are many contributors, but a major one is the fear of inadequacy. I feel inadequate facing issues or decisions without knowing how to handle them; anxiety results. I'm put on the spot to deal with certain of life's challenges and I draw a blank; anxiety rises. Tension, anger, and conflict often result.

"Training" can address this anxiety over inadequacy. Journey "with me" in handling certain discipline issues with the kids; be with me in certain social situations; role model to me how to deal with tense situations in public. Let's draw upon each other's strengths and help "train" each other.

▼ *Thanks, Lord, for my partner's strengths, which help train me for adequacy in all things.*

THE LOVE OF CHRIST CONSTRAINS ME

If you bite and devour one another, beware lest you be consumed by one another!
—GAL. 5:15

Some couples pressure each other by playing the "blame game": "I wouldn't be so critical if you'd quit watching TV." "I wouldn't watch so much TV if you'd be more affectionate." Each partner "pressures" the other to act in certain ways. We need training to do otherwise.

Marriage and family life suffer dramatically from the pressure to perform. This pressure often comes when emotional/relational needs are unmet and spouses stop trying to meet each other's needs. Affection is withheld. Emotional distancing takes place. Demanding, controlling, and "taking" soon replace grateful giving. Love becomes conditional, and the marriage is robbed of God's intended abundance.

God's Spirit comes to train us in His way—the way of giving, accepting, loving.

▼ *We're grateful, Father, that You've not left us to ourselves.*

IN THE TRIALS OF LIFE

That He who has begun a good work in you.
—PHIL. 1:6

I love the definition of *training*: journey with me to model God's way of facing life's issues. David and I both have been in training throughout our marriage. It seems when one of us is going through a journey of life the other is there to model stability or just to comfort and encourage the other.

When I'm in training for one of life's trials, I have the confidence that David will go through the trial with me. He always gives me comfort and support until the end.

Our marriage has been a journey in training others how not to make the mistakes we've made. We've often wondered why God has brought us down the paths He's chosen to bring us, but always on the other side we've understood. God can be trusted.

▼ *God causes all things to work together for good.*

A TRAINED HEART

*Solid food belongs to those who are mature .
. . who . . . have their senses trained to
discern both good and evil.*
—HEB. 5:14, NASB

*N*otice that training takes practice; it implies some progress and some defeat, maybe two steps forward and one back. Realizing this need for practice helps develop patience, patience with myself and patience with others.

Notice also the depth of training implied here as my "senses" can be trained in discernment. This is much more than becoming trained in a sport or hobby; much different from job training. This is a training within the human soul, which "sensitizes" my heart to the things of God; I become aware of His concerns, sharing in His burdens, attuned to His caring. It's here that sensitivity to a spouse originates—awareness, concern, and caring springing forth from a "trained" heart.

 Train my heart, O God, to discern You and to truly know my spouse.

"THE NARROW OPENING"

No chastening seems to be joyful for the present . . . afterward it yields the peaceable fruit of righteousness. —HEB. 12:11

A man watches a cocoon as the caterpillar inside painfully and tediously tries to force itself through a narrow opening. Thinking he will help the caterpillar, the man enlarges the opening, and the caterpillar emerges quickly and easily. But it has failed to develop properly and dies, never becoming the butterfly it was meant to be.

Marriage has its own narrow opening, doesn't it? Many difficult situations arise, and we are often tempted to avoid them or solve them superficially and quickly rather than painfully go right through them. That is why many couples stay malformed caterpillars rather than awe inspiring butterflies.

God wants to use our marriages to turn us into butterflies. Our marriages are a time of painful training that prepares us for flight. Anytime we refuse to go through those narrow openings, we are costing ourselves the ability to fly. Go through the narrow opening—and learn to fly.

▼ *God, help me to face difficulties in my marriage head on.*

BOOT CAMP

May the God of peace . . . make you
complete in every good work to do His will.
—HEB. 13:21

One couple described the first seven years of their marriage as "the great tribulation." Chris and I know what they mean. The early years of our marriage were pretty hard as we attempted to mature into a loving couple. We thought loving each other would come naturally. When it didn't, we did our fair share of finger pointing for who was to blame.

The early years of marriage can feel like you are in boot camp. The pain can be intense.

God, though, uses our marital pains and hurts to train us to be truly loving people. Marriage is clearly meant to be a training ground for the refinement of our character. God wants us to let the hardships increase our tolerance and strength.

Marriage isn't always meant to bring happiness, but it is meant to bring maturity.

▼ *God, thank You for using my marriage to train me to be more loving and selfless.*

LIFE TRAINING FROM GOAL SETTING

*Chastening . . . yields the peaceable fruit of
righteousness to those who have been trained
by it.*
                                                —HEB. 12:11

*W*here shall we invest our time, effort, and money?
Shall we participate in this activity? Should we support
this cause or project?

Without established goals, confusion and conflict often result in the face of these competing choices. But
with clearly defined and documented goals, decision
making is greatly simplified.

We often recommend that couples begin setting goals
annually. Usually a series of one-year goals works best.
Longer range goals, such as buying a house, should be
addressed but then broken down into what can be accomplished in a year. Many couples use the week between Christmas and New Year's as goal-setting time.
Some couples use the beginning of each school year as
their time to set goals. The important thing is to begin!

▼ *Father, guide us in goal setting for our marriage.*

TRUST—COMMITTED CONFIDENCE IN ANOTHER

The heart of her husband safely trusts her.
—PROV. 31:11

*W*alk up to the edge of all the light you have and then take one more step." This is how trust might be illustrated. Trust is never based on having all the answers, knowing all the facts, and therefore having a "dead cinch." It's based upon some answers and some facts, so it's not "blind" faith; but it wouldn't be trust if everything was known. We trust God having never seen Him; we trust His Son from reading of Him; we trust His Spirit though we cannot touch Him.

So it is with relational trust: I trust a partner not to betray me knowingly even though in their humanness, they will hurt me; I trust a partner with my most secret thoughts and feelings, believing they'll remain a secret just between us; I trust a partner with my deepest inadequacies and fears, hoping they'll protect me and never exploit me. Such trust when given and honored touches the depths of human intimacy.

▼ *What a joy it is, Father, to have a spouse in whom I can trust.*

I AM THAT I AM

Believe in the LORD your God, and you shall be established. —2 CHRON. 20:20

The great "I AM" of Scripture promises us a firm foundation. When Moses asked at the burning bush who he would say had sent him to deliver Israel, Jehovah's answer was "I AM WHO I AM" (Ex. 3:14). This name offers insights into the issue of trust. The first "I AM" is in a future tense, loosely translated "I am the one who will continue to be." The second "I am" is in a past tense, loosely translated "I always have been." Jehovah was saying: "I am the one who will continue to be who I always have been!" God's unchangeable nature, His consistency, prompts trust. He has been there for us mightily in the past; and since He never changes, He can be trusted with the future.

Teresa and I have come to experience aspects of this unchangeable consistency in our marriage relationship, each able to trust the other in a growing number of ways. This trust journey has been challenging but very rewarding.

▼ *Since He did not withhold His only Son from you, will He not freely, with Him, give you all things?*

TRUSTING UNCONDITIONALLY

My heart trusted in Him, and I am helped.
—PS. 28:7

I've had to really examine my own feelings in writing this. I've come to realize I've wanted to trust David with only the areas he's proven himself to be trustworthy. Trust is like love; it can't be conditional. Trusting David out of my feelings is wrong. I have to believe the best of him. I don't believe David ever consciously tries to hurt me, so when I withhold my trust, I've already judged his motives. What will be my focus in trusting him? I want to remember the positive. I do have a husband that I can share myself completely with. I can tell him everything and never be afraid of being made fun of. We can trust each other with our feelings so we don't have to play games. Trust doesn't always come easily, especially when we've been hurt by a spouse. Trust can be gained by choosing to believe in our spouse and think the best.

  Father, only as I keep my eyes on You and trust You can I totally trust my spouse.

ARE YOU FREE TO TRUST?

> *God is the God of all comfort, who will*
> *comfort us.*   —2 COR. 1:2–3

$\mathcal{T}$roy's earliest memories were of his acting silly to gain his drunken dad's attention. Ann's parents both worked. Tearfully, she described feeling closer to her housekeeper than to either of her parents. Neither really learned how to trust. Instead, both had become performers to gain approval and acceptance. Their performance journey had made them both successful but distant.

Often we set out to earn love and approval by performing. A child might seek attention by excelling in academics, athletics, popularity, or negatively through disruptive behavior. A spouse might feel the pressure of neglect and respond through increased activity and self-improvement programs, accompanied by complaining, blaming, and acting out. In each case the message is the same: "Notice me. I'm important."

As Ann and Troy grieved together and comforted each other, their trust was awakened and they found they had a caring spouse.

▼ *God, help us to share our pain and to comfort one another amid it.*

"IN GOD WE TRUST"

A wicked messenger falls into trouble
But a faithful ambassador brings health.
—PROV. 13:17

I don't trust you any farther than I can throw you!"
Some of us feel this way in marriage. Trust is delicate. It
can be destroyed gradually by small wrongs, and it can
be destroyed quickly with one huge wrong.

Given that all of us are imperfect and none of us is
totally trustworthy, how do we approach the issue of
trust in our marriages?

First, put your trust totally in God. He is worthy of
your complete trust. Trust your spouse but know ahead
of time he or she will fail you to some degree. We will
fail as well. Yet we can have enough trust in each other
to "glue" the relationship together.

When either spouse fails, we need to turn to God for
help. Our ultimate security is in Him, not in our spouse.

So, trust God with it all, and trust your spouse as
much as humanly possible.

▼ *God, help me put my complete trust in You, and help*
   me appropriately trust my spouse.

BLESSED ASSURANCE

Love . . . bears all things, believes all things,
hopes all things, endures all things.
—1 COR. 13:4, 7

Our apartment complex is full of non-Christians. We have gotten a view of how differently many non-Christians look at marriage.

One unmarried couple live together, too afraid of commitment to get married. Another couple, married for two years, recently separated for four months and just got back together. Still another married couple are trying marriage for the second time. They all leave the impression that marriage is expendable.

A lack of trust will destroy any marriage. You need to be able to depend on the commitment of your spouse. Yes, Chris and I have deeply hurt each other, and we probably will again in the future. But you don't give up. If there is no fear of your partner leaving, you can concentrate on making the marriage work.

Chris and I are in our marriage for the long haul, no matter who does what to whom. That trust makes all the difference in the world.

▼ *God, help my spouse and me to grow in our trust of*
each other, committed to building that trust through
good and bad times.

BUILDING BLOCKS OF TRUST

Do not trust in deceptive [empty] words.
—JER. 7:4 NASB

*T*eresa and I often note to couples that being vulnerable to discuss and address a growing number of topics is what builds a relationship. Many couples instead develop a list of "off-limit" topics—unable to discuss feelings, money, in-laws, sex, driving, golf, and so on. As this list of off-limit topics grows, marital distance grows and a shaky foundation is soon evident.

To address this issue and to encourage a deepening of trust in the relationship, we challenge couples to ask about intimacy: "In what ways can I make changes to improve our intimacy?" It's also important to review your confidentiality. Is your spouse secure that shared thoughts and feelings will remain confidential? Finally it's significant to consider your supportiveness. Can your partner count on your response to be empathetic and supportive? (Or do you "shoot down" ideas and negate feelings?)

These ingredients encourage vulnerability as trust is deepened and a growing list of topics is open for discussion.

 Keep us open, Father, deepening our vulnerable sharing on a broadening array of topics.

UNDERSTANDING—KNOWING WITHOUT JUDGING

Apply your heart to understanding.
—PROV. 2:2

*U*nderstanding is a matter of the heart just as knowledge is a matter of the head. To understand is to know intimately in experience; it is to become deeply acquainted with. Understanding begins with God, who knows all intimately. Man may look on the outside, but God looks on the heart. The psalmist speaks of His knowing my steps before I take them and my words before I speak them. He formed and fashioned me in my mother's womb and knows the number of my days in this life. He knows the intentions of my heart and the inner struggles of my flesh. And still He loves me. He's known me and not judged me. He knows my future failures and has not rejected me.

 O that someone knows me and still loves me; it meets a deep longing in my heart.

UNDERSTANDING THE ETERNAL

May the Lord give you understanding in all things.
                                        —2 TIM. 2:7

*W*e have an exciting promise concerning entering into God's "understanding." He knows all, being intimately acquainted with every past, present, and future happening. He reveals Himself as eternal in our temporal world.

To grasp and embrace this eternal perspective grants much understanding into this life. History must be viewed in this eternal context. Present temporal hardship will yield to eternal glory. We journey with couples as they come to understand our limited opportunities to touch eternal things: *God* is eternal, so we worship Him; *Scripture* is eternal, so we nourish our souls with it; *people* are eternal, so we love. God has put my marriage and family into an eternal context.

 Lord, I need Your eternal view of life, placing priority on things that will last forever.

WHY WON'T YOU FIX IT?

Who is wise and understanding among you?
Let him show by good conduct that his works
are done in the meekness of wisdom.
—JAMES 3:13

*F*rustration rose in me every time something in our home needed repair or I wanted to start a home project and David wouldn't help. I wanted us to work on projects together; his reply was always to hire someone to do it. I couldn't understand this.

David finally shared with me one night how he felt inadequate in the practical, how-to area. I then began to see that he wasn't just trying to get out of the work and I became more understanding. I also realized as he shared that I was comparing him to my father, who could fix everything; I was judging David, which wasn't fair.

▼ *Lord, help me not to compare, but to love my husband in an understanding way.*

OH, I SEE WHAT YOU MEAN

Understanding is a wellspring of life to him who has it.
—PROV. 16:22

$\mathcal{O}$rville and Wilbur Wright, after many failed attempts, successfully flew in December 1903. They excitedly telegraphed their sister Katherine, "We have actually flown 120 feet. We will be home for Christmas." She took their telegram to the local newspaper editor. He read it and said, "How nice. The boys will be home for Christmas."

That editor totally missed the point.

Do you find yourself "missing the point" in your marriage as you listen to your spouse? When you hear, "I've had a really rough day, especially when I went to the shopping mall," do you say, "Oh, you went to the mall? Did you get that shirt I asked you to?"

Marital intimacy means listening to your spouse at the deepest level possible in order to hear her or his deepest feelings, concerns, hopes, and fears.

 God, help me to understand my spouse in the deepest possible ways.

PUT ON MY SHOES AND WALK AROUND IN THEM A WHILE

Each of us should please his neighbor for his good to build him up. —ROM. 15:2

$\mathcal{J}$ ohn was a happily married man with a loving wife and children. He had been a Christian several years, and life was good. One morning, a young man called him at his office, claiming to be John's twenty-year-old son. The young man explained he had been adopted as a baby and had for the last two years been searching for his biological parents. Would John be willing to meet with him?

John was stunned. He never knew his girlfriend had been pregnant when they broke up. Now, all he could think about was whether or not this would destroy his marriage. He promised to call his newfound son later with the decision about whether or not to see him, and hung up. After much prayer and counsel from a trusted friend John sat his wife down and told her the whole story.

Without hesitation, John's wife threw her arms around him and said she understood all the pain he must have been going through. She told him that she loved him and was there to help him. His wife's understanding response caused his love and respect for her to grow.

▼ *God, thank You that marriage is a place where pain can be shared and understanding can be offered.*

DOES ANYONE UNDERSTAND ME?

Do you not yet understand?
—MATT. 15:17

*W*e often ask couples about who really "knew" them as they were growing up. Very often the sad and tragic answer is that no one really did—life went on and surface issues were dealt with, but no one really entered their world to know them. This is what understanding is all about. Each of us has a need to be understood by people we care about.

In Teresa's and my journey to better understanding each other, we've focused on several practical issues. We ask about opinions, ideas, and dreams, to better understand why each holds these as important. We care about feelings of all kinds—joy and hope, sadness and anxiety—and accept them and don't judge them. We empathize with each other's feelings and don't analyze them. We explore childhood reflections. These will give insight into our life "journey," some of our needs, and possibly some of our hurts. And finally we accept weaknesses, cutting each other a little slack over imperfections.

▼ *Father, lead us into the depths of understanding each other.*

FELLOWSHIP, FRIENDSHIP AND PASSION

They shall become one flesh.
—GEN. 2:24

*I*n our counseling, teaching, and writing, we refer to God's plan for marriage intimacy as the freedom to share all of oneself with one's spouse—spirit, soul, and body. It's our prayer that your marriage be challenged by the mystery of God's plan for two becoming one.

It's our hope that you walk as two saints sharing fellowship; two recipients of transforming grace living in the awe and wonder of being loved by their Creator (John 1:15); two mere humans experiencing together the inexpressible joy of being children of God, partakers of the divine nature (2 Pet. 1:4); two aliens walking in this world, but not of this world (1 Pet. 2:11; John 17:16), laboring together as ambassadors for Christ; being transformed together into His image (2 Cor. 3:18; 5:20); longing together for His return (1 John 3:2).

It's our prayer that you become very best friends; two hearts stirred to cherish each other, experiencing together life's joys and struggles—sometimes up and sometimes down. It's our desire that you enjoy the specialness of two lovers sharing passion; physical excitement, expectation, and arousal, prompting a desire to become one flesh (Gen. 2:24).

▼ *Father, bless our journey together with many intimate moments.*

About the Authors

Dr. David Ferguson is client services director of the Minirth-Meier Tunnel & Wilson Clinic in Austin, Texas, and executive director of the Center for Marriage and Family Intimacy. He has a doctorate of philosophy from Oxford Graduate School and has done post-graduate work at Dallas Theological Seminary.

Teresa Ferguson is co-editor of the Marriage and Family Intimacy newsletter and speaks to thousands of women around the country with the Great Hills Retreat Ministry.

David and Teresa have raised three children and live in Austin, Texas.

Dr. Chris Thurman is a licensed psychologist who maintains an active counseling practice at the Minirth-Meier Tunnell & Wilson Clinic. Chris is author of the bestseller *The Lies We Believe* and *The Truths We Must Believe.* Chris speaks nationwide on such topics as "straight" (truthful) thinking, stress and anger management, personal excellence, and self-esteem. He received his Ph.D. in counseling psychology from the University of Texas at Austin.

Holly Thurman received a B.A. in history from the University of Texas at Austin. Holly is active in Bible Study Fellowship as well as church and school activities.

Chris and Holly are the parents of three children and live in Austin, Texas.

Other Books in the
Minirth-Meier Clinic Series

Anger Workbook
   Dr. Les Carter

The Father Book
   Dr. Frank Minirth, Dr. Brian Newman, Dr. Paul Warren

Imperative People
   Dr. Les Carter

The Intimacy Factor
   Dr. David Stoop, Jan Stoop

Kids Who Carry Our Pain
   Dr. Robert Hemfelt, Dr. Paul Warren

The Lies We Believe
   Dr. Chris Thurman

Love Hunger: Recovery from Food Addiction
   Dr. Frank Minirth, Dr. Paul Meier, Dr. Robert Hemfelt,
   Dr. Sharon Sneed

Love Hunger Action Plan
   Dr. Sharon Sneed

The Love Hunger Weight-Loss Workbook
   Dr. Frank Minirth, Dr. Paul Meier, Dr. Robert Hemfelt,
   Dr. Sharon Sneed

Love Is a Choice
   Dr. Robert Hemflet, Dr. Frank Minirth, Dr. Paul Meier

Love Is a Choice Workbook
   Dr. Robert Hemfelt, Dr. Frank Minirth, Dr. Paul Meier,
   Dr. Brian Newman, Dr. Deborah Newman

Passages of Marriage Series
New Love
Realistic Love
Steadfast Love
Renewing Love
Transcendent Love
   Dr. Frank and Mary Alice Minirth, Drs. Brian and Deborah
   Newman, Dr. Robert and Susan Hemfelt

Passages of Marriage Study Guide Series
New Love Study Guide
Realistic Love Study Guide
Steadfast Love Study Guide
Renewing Love Study Guide
Transcendent Love Study Guide
   Dr. Frank and Mary Alice Minirth, Drs. Brian and Deborah
   Newman, Dr. Robert and Susan Hemfelt

The Path to Serenity
   Dr. Robert Hemfelt, Dr. Frank Minirth, Dr. Richard Fowler,
   Dr. Paul Meier

Please Let Me Know You, God
   Dr. Larry Stephens

The Quest
   Kevin J. Brown, Ray Mitsch

Steps to a New Beginning
   Sam Shoemaker, Dr. Frank Minirth, Dr. Richard Fowler,
   Dr. Brian Newman, Dave Carder

The Thin Disguise
   Pam Vredevelt, Dr. Deborah Newman, Harry Beverly,
   Dr. Frank Minirth

Thngs That Go Bump in the Night
   Dr. Paul Warren, Dr. Frank Minirth

The Truths We Must Believe
   Dr. Chris Thurman

Together on a Tightrope
   Dr. Richard Fowler, Rita Schweitz

Hope for the Perfectionist
   Dr. David Stoop

For general information about other Minirth-Meier Clinic
branch offices, counseling services, educational resources and
hospital programs, call toll-free 1-800-545-1819. National
Headquarters: (214) 669-1733 (800) 229-3000.